I0825324

日本のお漬物と発酵の世界

The *Japanese* art of

PICKLING & FERMENTING

YOKO NAKAZAWA

Smith Street Books

CONTENTS

INTRODUCTION

はじめに

Pickling and fermenting is more than preserving food. It connects the past, present and the future. It also connects people and places. Local vegetables, cultivated in different regions, carry with them the knowledge and experience of those who have grown them. Through generations, the seeds of those vegetables are preserved, passed down and grown. Knowledge about how to grow each unique variety, respond to the local climate, as well as other region-specific wisdom, is passed from elders to the young, linking both the seeds and this local knowledge to the future. These carefully cultivated vegetables are then preserved as pickles, extending their life as food.

Many pickles can be stored for long periods. When freshly made, they have a vibrant flavour, while those aged for a long time develop a depth that makes them even more delicious. A great example is umeboshi (salted plums). In some Japanese traditions, a hundred umeboshi are prepared as a gift for a newborn, with the intention of the child enjoying one each year on their birthday. Eating a single umeboshi every year becomes a ritual of gratitude – for life, for the parents who made them, and for nature itself, which nurtured the plums. With each umeboshi, one hopes for health for the following year. Even after the parents have passed on, this gift continues. What a wonderful present.

Japan is good at preserving the past to enjoy in the present and for the future. Not only pickles, but culture, tradition, style, aesthetics, architecture, clothing, festivals and philosophy.

In Japan, all these things are deeply connected to nature. The country has distinct seasons, and its mild climate, along with its geographical features, allow for a wide variety of plants to flourish. The distance between mountains and sea is relatively short, and snowmelt flows through streams, providing clean drinking water almost everywhere. This water is life-giving and healing. Numerous natural springs bubble up from the ground, and people bathe in hot spring water to heal illness and relieve fatigue.

Thanks to this abundant, pure water, rice cultivation has thrived, making it a staple food and leading to the development of many fermented seasonings based on rice. Japanese sake, too, owes its quality to pure water. Because of the bounty of this resource, cooking methods that rely on water, such as boiling and steaming, are common. The high humidity in the air also encourages the growth of beneficial molds, which are used to make a wide variety of fermented foods. Nature provides other blessings too, like wild mountain vegetables that bring unique flavours. Truly, Japan is a 'Land of Bountiful Grains', blessed with water in every sense.

This abundance of water also brings danger. Frequent typhoons and heavy rains can lead to flooding. While hot springs offer comfort, the presence of active volcanoes poses constant threats, and earthquakes are also common. Nature holds an overwhelming power that is beyond human control, evoking both reverence and fear. Life in Japan exists amidst a rich but challenging natural environment, where people fear natural disasters. In such a country, the practice of 'preserving' has long been valued. To create preserved foods is, in a sense, to cultivate the strength to endure and survive.

Japan's seasons are often described as having four distinct phases, but in fact, they are broadly divided into 24 mini seasons, which can be further separated into early, mid and late periods. This means that the year can actually be broken down into 72 seasons. Each of these periods has a name that reflects a natural phenomenon or the behaviour of particular plants and animals. Thus, the seasons shift every five days, continually moving forward. (In Melbourne, Australia, near to where I live now, they say you experience all four seasons in a single day! This is quite different from the Japanese sense of seasons, and even after more than a decade here, my body and mind still struggle to adapt.)

Just as the mountain streams flow quickly, ever forward, people in Japan seem to feel an innate sense of this steady progression – at least, that's how I felt. Cherry blossoms bloom with breathtaking beauty, but it's fleeting, ephemeral. They may be gone by tomorrow. Nothing remains the same, and nature teaches us that everything is in constant flux.

Among all this, pickles are truly magical – they capture a moment in time and carry it into the future. Not only do they preserve, but they grow ever more delicious, deep and complex, bridging the past and the future like a time machine. Thanks to the knowledge and experience of those who came before us, we can still make pickles today that won't spoil even after a hundred years at room temperature. I am filled with gratitude.

Since I was little, I've been eating pickles made from different vegetables in various ways. Every meal – whether breakfast, lunch or dinner – always included some kind of pickles on our table, and it was natural for me to munch on them every day. Of course, pickles were also included in bento boxes (whether it was a homemade bento, an Ekiben from the station, or even a convenience-store bento). For me, pickles are an essential food item, and if there aren't any on the table, I somehow feel like something is missing.

Our family was almost self-sufficient in vegetables; Dad grew seasonal produce in our garden, and Mum would prepare it in various ways, ensuring we never tired of the same thing. She would cook the vegetables or turn them into pickles, all while discussing things like, 'Maybe this one fermented a bit too long', or 'This one turned out delicious!' Through these simple home-cooked meals, we enjoyed the bounty of our garden, savoured the changing seasons, and preserved food through pickling. In that sense, I guess I received a kind of pickle education from an early age.

In Japan, pickles are usually made using local produce, resulting in a wide variety of regional pickles. Given the country's long, narrow shape, each region has traditional vegetables suited to its climate, which are then often preserved. They also make great souvenirs (I believe you can buy pickles as souvenirs almost anywhere in Japan!). When friends travel to different regions, they might bring back pickles as gifts. In these moments, we'd enjoy discussing, 'This one was a gift from so-and-so; they went to such-and-such place', or 'This one was sent from our neighbour's hometown; that area is famous for red turnips.' As we tried these unique flavours, we'd express our preferences, saying things like, 'This tastes just like Kyoto!' or 'Ah, this is definitely from Yamagata.' Pickles not only add variety to the dining table but also spark conversations. By the way, as I'm writing this introduction to my book, I'm making a brief visit to Japan. Just today, I went to a hot spring, and even at the shop there, they were selling pickles made from rare vegetables.

For me, pickles announce the new season. They reflect the flavours of time – spring's wild vegetables, early summer's plums, summer's cucumbers, autumn's chrysanthemum flowers, and, of course, the winter scents of yuzu and thick daikon radish. When we ate these seasonal pickles for the first time each year, we'd say, 'Oh, it's that season already', and celebrate and appreciate its arrival. These memories are not just about the pickles themselves but also about the scenes of my parents making them with our home-grown vegetables and the state of our garden. Particularly, the process of making umeboshi, winter's takuan (pickled daikon) – and the wonderful aroma that filled the room during the process – the sight of beautifully drying wombok (Chinese cabbage) spread across the garden (and the conversations with my parents as they worried about the weather), and the sight of heavy pickle stones stacked on barrels. All these elements are vividly intertwined with each pickle, creating a strong sense of seasonal tradition within me.

My mother often said, 'Nothing beats freshness.' Japanese home cooking, which doesn't rely heavily on spices or rich sauces, reflects the taste of fresh vegetables directly. Pickles are no exception. They taste great because of the freshness of the produce. On top of that, the knowledge accumulated over centuries of how best to preserve food to enhance flavour, makes them even more delicious. Fermentation also significantly boosts the nutritional value. I can't help but call it the magic of pickles.

Pickling was originally a way to preserve vegetables, especially in regions with harsh winters and heavy snowfall. My mother, who is from the northern region of Japan, often told me stories about how valuable pickles were as a source of vegetables when fresh ones were unavailable in winter. People would eat pickled leafy vegetables to supplement their vitamins while waiting for the snow to melt and spring to arrive. This is why so many varieties of pickles are made from leafy greens. In cold regions like Hokkaido, Tohoku, Hokuriku and other coastal areas, it's also common to pickle fish. These regions, known for their fresh seafood, make large catches of seasonal fish, leading to preservation methods like drying and fermenting for long-term storage.

I once stumbled upon a shop specialising in fish pickled in rice bran while travelling on the Izu Peninsula. There, they grilled your chosen pickled fish over a brazier or hibachi, and I was amazed by the deep flavour. The usual fishy smell was gone, replaced by an incredibly rich umami taste. This too, I believe, is an example of how people in fish-abundant regions developed preservation techniques. Travelling introduces you to various flavours, offering a contrast to home-cooked meals and adding excitement to daily life.

In this book, I've included many of the home-style pickles I've eaten since I was a child. These are simple, everyday pickles made from a variety of vegetables. They range from quick pickles made with sweet vinegar to traditional, seasonal fermented pickles. They may look modest, but their flavours are deep and rich. And don't worry about following the recipes exactly – you don't have to! Close enough is good enough. What's important about pickles is that there's no 'one right way' to make them. The results can vary depending on the condition of the ingredients, the weather, and even the household or region. Feel free to substitute local ingredients from your country or region, adjust the saltiness or sourness to your liking and make them your own.

I hope you'll enjoy adding these pickles to your daily meals, knowing they'll surely contribute to your health. Plus, having some pickles on hand is incredibly convenient when you're wondering, what should I make for dinner tonight? Just a small addition of pickles can elevate the presentation of a dish, and they can even enhance the flavour of your main course.

I hope your pickle-making journey brings you joy.

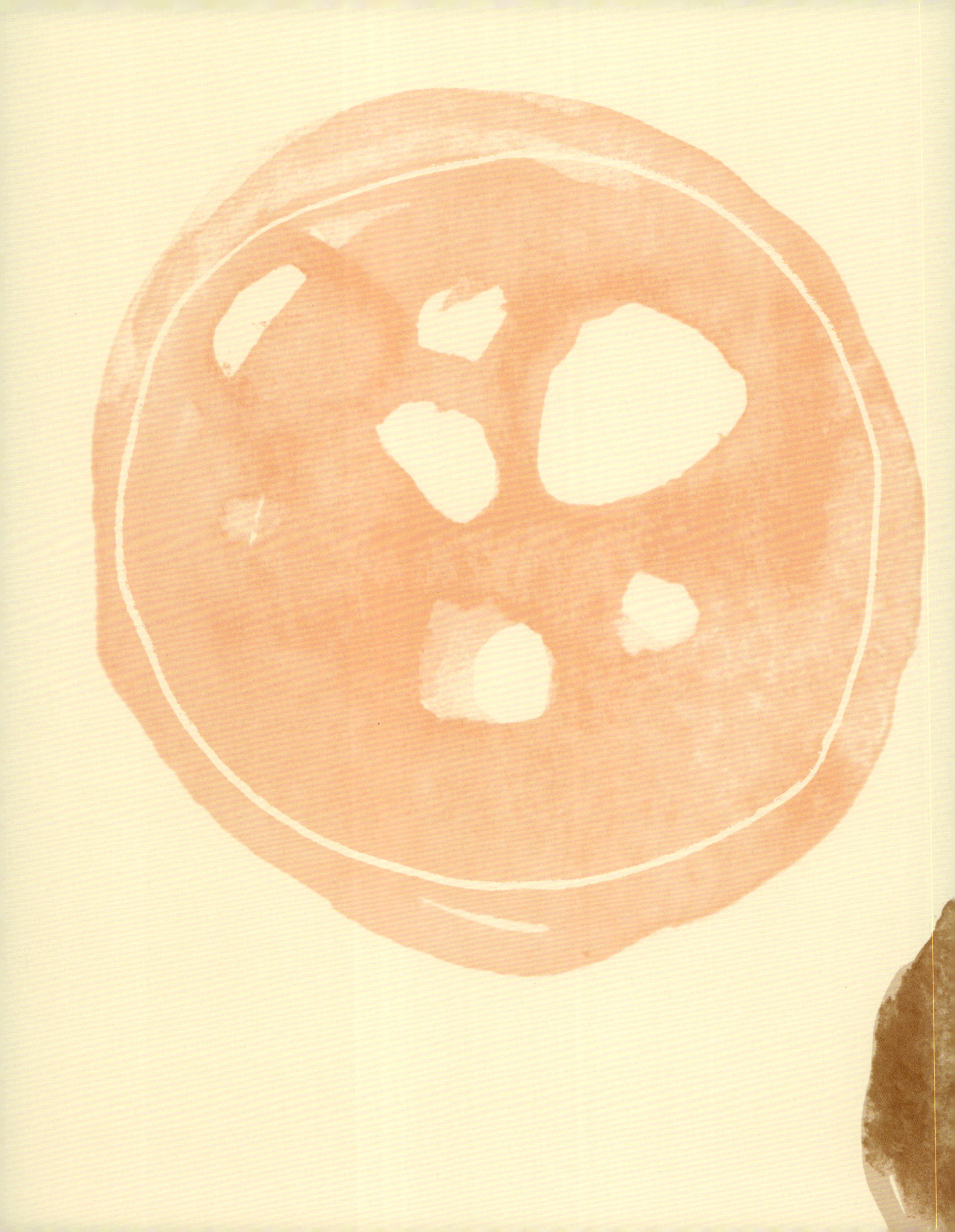

GETTING STARTED

お漬物の世界へようこそ

Making pickles doesn't come with strict rules. The most basic ingredients are simply vegetables and salt. You don't need any special tools either – there are plenty of pickles you can make with just what you have at home. Start casually by using vegetables you already have.

In this book, I often haven't included 'makes' or 'serves'. It doesn't really matter how much you make or how much produce you use. Just check the weight of the vegetables and apply enough salt based on percentages as shown in the recipes. But if you get used to it, you don't even have to do that. I must confess, I don't calculate salt amounts most of the time!

People often ask, 'How should I eat pickles?' but there are no rules for that, either. Serve them as a side dish, use them as a topping, or enjoy them with cheese and crackers. There are endless ways to enjoy pickles – it's the perfect opportunity to get creative!

BEYOND PRESERVATION: DISCOVERING JAPANESE OTSUKEMONO

奥深いお漬物の世界

In Japan, the world of otsukemono ('pickles' in Japanese) is incredibly diverse, with more than 600 known varieties (some say there are as many as 4000!). Otsukemono were originally made as a way to preserve food, and they were particularly common in colder regions, especially in snowy areas. Today, across Japan, a wide array of traditional vegetables are fermented or immersed in various pickling bases. The diversity of otsukemono is remarkable, deeply reflecting the regional characteristics of each area.

In this book, I share a selection of otsukemono that I often make myself and those I grew up eating. To make the recipes accessible to readers worldwide, I've chosen vegetables that are widely and easily available. The book is divided into ten chapters, each dedicated to a specific type of otsukemono.

From simple and quick salt-pickled Asazuke (see page 72) to more involved fermented otsukemono steeped in tradition, there's something here for everyone – whether you're a beginner pickler or fermentation enthusiast. While the authentic fermented pickles do require time and effort, the reward is unparalleled flavour that you simply won't find in supermarkets. They offer the joy of tasting evolving flavours and textures as time goes by. Some, like the pickling bed used for Nukazuke (see page 186), can even be passed down through generations, embodying a profound sense of heritage and continuity.

Making otsukemono isn't just about the end result; it's about rediscovering the joy of crafting something by hand, nurturing it as it develops, and embracing the ambiguity of a process without absolute answers. It's about reconnecting with nature and finding harmony within it. Through pickling, I hope you'll experience these joys and more.

For example, lightly salted otsukemono, or those made with sweet vinegar, can be enjoyed relatively soon after making them (from around 20 minutes to overnight). They are quick and easy to make, so you don't have to prepare that many at once. Takuan (see page 233) or Narazuke (see page 120), on the other hand, require several weeks of preparation and a fair bit of effort. It's a once-a-year thing. In these instances I make a big portion and enjoy a few slices every day until I've consumed all the otsukemono.

Whatever you make, my advice is to use fresh seasonal produce and good-quality seasonings. As pickles are very simple, the quality and flavour of these basic ingredients really matters.

WHAT ARE OTSUKEMONO, BY THE WAY?
お漬物って何ですか？

Otsukemono are vegetables, and sometimes fish, that are preserved by being soaked or fermented with salt or Japanese fermented seasonings such as miso, tamari or vinegar. The resulting flavour varies depending on the type of vegetable, the seasoning used for pickling and the fermentation period. Most pickles are savoury and are often eaten as a side dish with rice. When eaten this way, they amazingly make the rice taste twice or even three times as good. Otsukemono are also commonly served as accompaniments with morning or afternoon tea and, of course, they pair wonderfully with Japanese tea.

As you can see, otsukemono are an essential part of Japanese meals. They are an important dish in the basic structure of Japanese cuisine. The simplest form of Japanese cuisine, known as *ichiju issai* (one soup, one side dish), consists of rice, miso soup and pickles. This trio creates a very simple, yet complete, Japanese meal. My breakfast often follows this style. Occasionally, eggs or natto (fermented soybeans) are added for protein, but otsukemono are always included. Though simple, the presence of pickles adds colour and creates a nutritionally balanced meal.

WHAT CAN YOU PICKLE AND FERMENT?

何を漬ける？

Almost any vegetable can be made into otsukemono: cucumbers, carrots, turnips, daikon, cabbage, wombok (Chinese cabbage), cauliflower ... Whether it's a vegetable you love, one you've harvested from your garden or have been gifted from a neighbour, or some delicious-looking produce from the farmers' market, you can try pickling them all. If you shop seasonally, you can buy produce at a reasonable price. Once pickled, the nutritional value of the vegetable increases, and it becomes even more delicious. Most importantly, its shelf life improves. Pickles were originally made to preserve vegetables – the fact that they taste better and become more nutritious is just an added bonus. So even before the scientific understanding of microorganisms, pickles were contributing to people's health. How wonderful!

HOW DOES PICKLING & FERMENTING PRESERVE FOOD?

どうしてお漬物って保存が効くの？

When making otsukemono, there are five key factors of preservation to consider: salt concentration, moisture, oxygen, temperature and acidity.

SALT CONCENTRATION: A high salt concentration prevents many microorganisms from growing.

MOISTURE: Removing moisture from vegetables is important for preservation. This can be achieved by drying the vegetables or sprinkling them with salt to draw out the liquid in their cells (osmotic pressure).

OXYGEN: By burying the vegetables in a pickling bed or seasoning liquid, you maintain an oxygen-free environment.

TEMPERATURE: A lower temperature is better, especially for long-fermented otsukemono, so pickling and fermenting are often more common in colder regions. In warmer areas, people often use refrigerators or make pickles in the cooler winter months.

ACIDITY: Using vinegar or encouraging lactic acid fermentation increases the acidity, which helps preserve the vegetables.

Additionally, sometimes the power of the sun can be utilised: exposing pickles, particularly umeboshi and umezu, to sunlight helps sterilise them, while sun-drying extends their preservation period. I also sterilise my containers this way.

— ***TIPS:*** When making pickles, be sure to wash your hands thoroughly and dry them with a clean towel before starting.

Also, when taking pickles out of a container to eat, use clean chopsticks or a fork. Don't use anything that has already been in your mouth. Small things like this can affect the preservation period of the otsukemono.

WHAT'S THE DIFFERENCE BETWEEN PICKLING & FERMENTING?

お漬物って発酵食品ですか？

In relation to microorganisms, pickles can be categorised into two types: fermented and non-fermented pickles. In Japan, both are referred to as 'otsukemono'.

Examples of fermented pickles include shibazuke and nukazuke, both of which you'll find in this book. Many fermented pickles utilise lactic acid bacteria, which thrive and make the food more acidic, preventing the growth of harmful bacteria and improving preservation. Lactic acid bacteria prefer environments without oxygen (anaerobic), so when food is salted and weighted down, blocking the air, harmful bacteria cannot survive, and only the lactic acid bacteria proliferate.

Among these fermented pickles, Nukazuke (see page 186) is particularly special because it involves not just lactic acid bacteria but also yeasts, butyric acid bacteria and other microorganisms, which, together, create a complex flavour. Butyric acid bacteria produce butyric acid, a short-chain fatty acid that is said to promote gut health, making nukazuke a particularly beneficial and health-boosting otsukemono.

Non-fermented pickles are those made in environments where microorganisms cannot thrive, such as salt pickles or vinegar pickles. Vinegar prevents the growth of microorganisms due to its acidity. Unlike fermented pickles that become acidic through lactic acid bacteria, the acidity of vinegar pickles comes directly from the vinegar itself, improving preservation. Take umeboshi, for example. Although umeboshi is capable of long-term preservation, it is not a fermented pickle because no microorganisms are involved in the process. The high acidity from the citric acid in the plums and the high salt concentration prevent microorganisms from thriving in this environment.

Even among non-fermented pickles, some use fermented seasonings, such as miso, soy sauce or fermented byproducts like sake lees, to make otsukemono. These include misozuke, kasuzuke and tamarizuke, and they are made using pickling beds of the fermented seasonings, which provide a rich flavour. Japan has a variety of these pickling beds (tsuke doko), and their richness contributes to the variety of Japanese otsukemono.

Types of pickling beds (tsuke doko)

Miso, vinegar, koji, soy sauce, mirin, mirin lees, sake lees, shio-koji and shoyu-koji are all examples of fermented seasonings. Depending on the type of pickling bed, the otsukemono are referred to as:

- Miso – **Misozuke** (Miso pickles)
- Vinegar – **Suzuke** (Vinegar pickles)
- Koji – **Kojizuke** (Koji pickles)
- Soy sauce – **Shoyu zuke** (Soy sauce pickles)
- Mirin – **Mirin zuke** (Mirin pickles)
- Mirin lees – **Mirin kasuzuke** (Mirin lees pickles)
- Sake lees – **Kasuzuke** (Sake lees pickles)
- Shio-koji – **Shio kojizuke** (Salt koji pickles)
- Shoyu-koji – **Shoyu kojizuke** (Soy sauce koji pickles)

Also, even within the same type of pickle, the length of the pickling time can influence whether they're called asazuke (lightly pickled) or furuzuke (aged pickled). Asazuke have a beautiful colour, with a fresh, salad-like taste. Furuzuke often have a deeper, more subdued colour and a strong, traditional pickle flavour. The acidity and saltiness tend to become much stronger over time. Some people prefer asazuke, while others prefer furuzuke. It's a matter of personal preference, and that's what makes otsukemono wonderful.

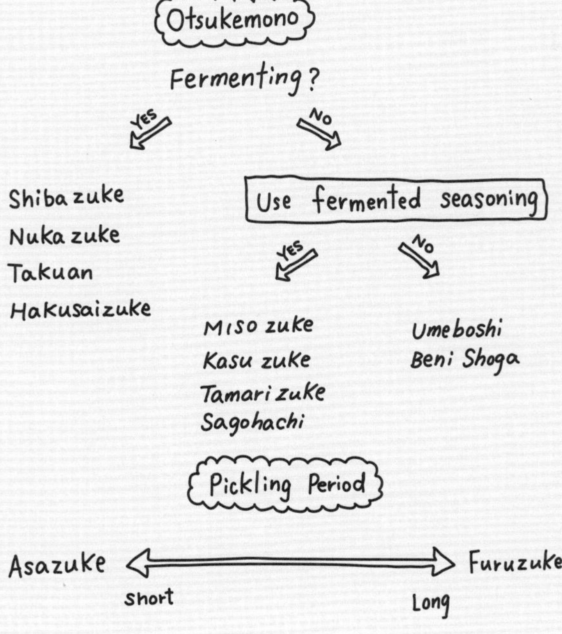

JAPANESE PICKLING EQUIPMENT

お漬物づくりに必要な道具

Below is a guide to the equipment I use to make otsukemono. Although not exhaustive, this equipment will make your pickling journey easier and give your otsukemono a greater chance of success.

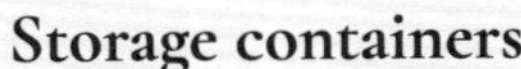

Storage containers

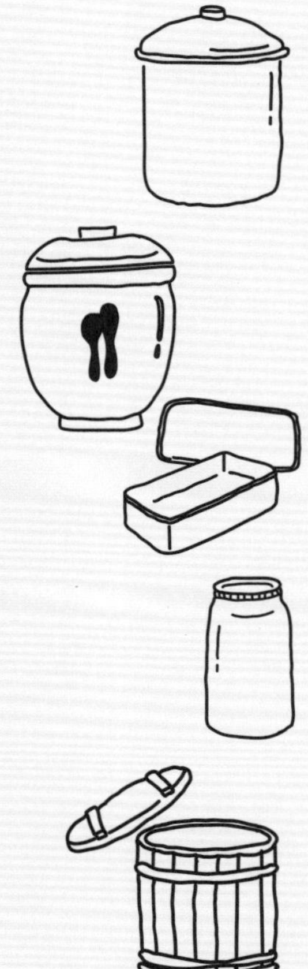

Any container that is resistant to acids and salt and has a lid can be used. Avoid materials, such as aluminium and copper, which are vulnerable to acids and salt. A container with a wide mouth for adding and removing vegetables is the most practical.

– ENAMEL CONTAINERS

Lightweight and easy to use, when making larger batches of pickles a bucket-shaped enamel container is ideal. For pickles stored in the refrigerator, small enamel containers are best. Be careful not to drop or scratch your enamel containers, as they can rust. Avoid using metal scrubs.

– GLASS STORAGE JARS, SEALED JARS

Jars are best for making pickles with a lot of liquid. It's nice to see the contents from the outside, and a shape that allows for the easy removal of vegetables is useful. When storing pickles long term, avoid metal lids, or place baking paper in between the jar and the lid. If making pickles that require the jar to be turned upside down (such as the radish pickles on page 63), sealed jars are perfect to prevent spills.

– PICKLING CROCKS (EARTHENWARE)

I recommend pickling crocks for their resistance against odours and acids. They also minimise temperature fluctuations, which is an advantage. However, they are heavy. It's best to use ones that have a cylindrical shape.

– FOOD-GRADE PLASTIC CONTAINERS

These containers are resistant to salt and acids, and are lighter and easier to handle than some heavier containers.

– PICKLING WOODEN BARRELS

Often used for nukazuke (rice bran pickles) or takuan (pickled daikon) in Japan, wooden barrels provide good ventilation and absorb moisture, plus microbes can live in the wood, which can give your otsukemono a unique flavour. I like the look of wooden barrels too – they have a certain charm. On the downside, controlling the moisture can be tricky, and there might be concerns about odour leakage. Sometimes insects are attracted to them.

– ZIPLOCK BAGS – COMPOSTABLE

Compostable ziplock bags are very convenient when pickling small quantities or for otsukemono that only require short pickling periods. When laid flat, the bag makes it easy to distribute a small amount of liquid to cover the vegetables. Compostable bags are also an environmentally friendly choice.

– INNER LID

After filling a storage container with ingredients, use an inner lid before adding the weight. This ensures that the weight is distributed evenly. A lid slightly smaller than the container works best, and a flat plate can be used as an alternative.

Scales

Use scales to measure your ingredients. I use analogue scales to weigh vegetables, and digital scales for salt and sugar, and other ingredients where only a small amount is required.

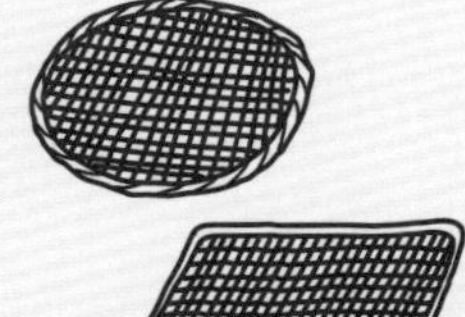

Flat Zaru (Bamboo Colander/Basket/Sieve)

Zaru are baskets or sieves used for draining, drying or serving food. There are two main types: deep, round zaru, like colanders, and flat zaru, which are wide and shallow, like trays. Flat zaru, often made of bamboo, are especially useful for sun-drying vegetables when pickling, draining and cooling blanched vegetables. You can find them in Asian stores.

Netted Drying Basket

Also used for drying produce, a netted drying basket is handy when it's windy outside, plus it helps protect against insects and birds. You can buy them cheaply from Japanese stores and online.

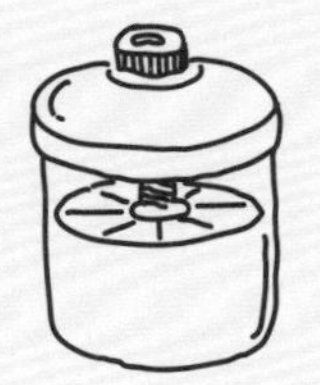

Japanese Pickle Press

This simple tool is used to apply pressure to pickled vegetables, helping them release moisture and absorb seasonings more effectively. It typically consists of a container with a weighted or screw-down lid to press the ingredients.

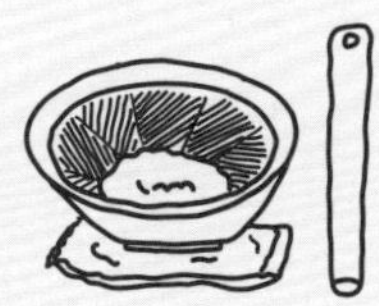

Suribachi & Surikogi

A suribachi is a Japanese mortar: a ceramic bowl with a textured interior designed for grinding and blending ingredients efficiently. A suribachi is typically used with a surikogi, which is a wooden pestle. In pickling, they are often used to mix fermenting pastes.

— *TIP:* When using unstable-shaped weights, such as bottles, it's very handy to have two buckets of the same size. Put the vegetables in the first bucket and the bottle in the second. Place the bottle-containing bucket on top of the bucket with the vegetables in it. Although it might not look great, it works effectively!

Weights

Adding weights during the pickling process quickly removes moisture from vegetables and ensures that their surface is covered in their own moisture. Once the liquid submerges the vegetables, you know everything is working as it should. For large weights, I often use a rock from my garden, thoroughly cleaned and sanitised with boiling water. Large bottles filled with liquid also work, as do workout dumbbells. However, weights that aren't flat on the bottom or weights that are tall may not be stable, so placing them in a bucket to prevent them from tipping over or avoid them getting wet from pickle juice is a good solution (see Tip). For smaller weights, you can use an appropriately sized plate or a jam jar – anything you already have in the kitchen.

Sterilising

It's important to sterilise and disinfect all equipment before use. I usually sterilise items by pouring boiling water over them. For heat-resistant glass containers, I place them in the oven at 100°C (210°F) for about 10 minutes.

For larger items that don't fit in the oven, I disinfect them with high-proof alcohol (35 per cent or higher). I spray the alcohol directly onto the items or use a paper towel soaked in alcohol to wipe them.

Also, don't forget to sterilise inner lids, lids and weights that will come into direct contact with your ingredients.

On sunny days, it's even better to sterilise items by sun-drying them for a couple of hours. It also brings a peaceful feeling. Pickling and peace.

SOME USEFUL TECHNIQUES
基本のテクニック

In this section I will explain some of the techniques I use in this book.

Massaging vegetables

You can massage vegetables either in a bowl or in a compostable ziplock bag. For smaller amounts, using a ziplock bag is more effective because the pickling liquid coats the vegetables more evenly.

MASSAGING VEGETABLES IN A BOWL

Chop the vegetables, then place them in a bowl with a sprinkling of salt (or the amount specified in the recipe). Knead the vegetables by gently pressing and massaging them with your hands, until moisture is released. Place a plate or a similar weight on top to lightly press them down.

MASSAGING VEGETABLES USING A COMPOSTABLE SEALABLE BAG

Chop the vegetables and place them in a compostable ziplock bag, along with the salt. Seal the bag, pressing out as much as air as possible, then work the vegetables with your hands, pressing and massaging gently.

Cuts for vegetables

Try the following Japanese knife cuts when preparing your otsukemono. These techniques increase the surface area of the vegetable you're cutting, making it easier for flavours to soak in and for seasonings to adhere. Plus, incorporating different chopping styles can change the texture of your otsukemono, adding variety and interest.

RANGIRI (IRREGULAR CUT)

Rangiri is often used to cut root vegetables when making soup and pickles. Starting from one end of your vegetable, make a diagonal cut, then rotate the vegetable about 90 degrees and chop again. Repeat the process to create evenly sized irregular cuts.

JABARA (SNAKE TUMMY CUT)

This cut is often used for cucumbers and the end result looks a bit like an accordion. Simply score the cucumber with fine diagonal cuts on one side (or both sides).

TATAKI (HIT)

This 'cut' is also used for cucumbers but it's not actually a cut at all. We hit the cucumber with a piece of wood, such as a rolling pin. Hitting the cucumber smashes it into pieces and creates a rough surface.

MY JAPANESE PICKLES PANTRY

お漬物づくりで使う調味料

Otsukemono are made with simple ingredients. Seasonings are vital in shaping their flavour, so it's important to choose them carefully, paying attention to their method of production, quality and taste. I highly recommend using fermented seasonings aged using traditional techniques.

Soy sauce

As well as assisting preservation, soy sauce adds aroma and umami to pickles. You can use tamari soy sauce or regular soy sauce, but I like to use miso tamari – the liquid you get when you make miso paste. Miso tamari has a much milder taste.

Soy sauce (or tamari) should be made using only soybeans, wheat and salt, so choose one without any additives or colours. I also recommend seeking out one made using traditional methods.

Miso

The recipes in this book use long-fermented brown rice miso, which has been fermented for more than a year. I use homemade miso but you can use any miso you like. If your miso has a mild flavour and you'd like it to be saltier, try adding a little salt or more miso paste. Miso made using traditional methods is superior to mass-produced miso.

Mirin

I recommend using traditional slow-fermented hon mirin, also known as 'true mirin'. Other mirin-style seasonings often contain added sugar, sweeteners or syrups (check the ingredients list on the back of the bottle). Hon mirin has an amazing natural sweetness and umami derived from rice koji.

Rice koji

Rice koji is steamed rice that has been inoculated with koji mold (*Aspergillus oryzae*) and fermented. It is a key ingredient in Japanese fermentation, used to make miso, sake, mirin and vinegar as well as fermented seasonings such as shio koji and ama koji. I use it to make Kabura sushi (see page 144), Sagohachi 3:5:8 zuke (see page 138) and Sanshozuke (see page 142). Dried rice koji can be found at Japanese grocery stores and online.

大和言

Sake kasu (sake lees)

Sake kasu is the leftover residue from pressing sake. It has a wonderful flavour and has been used for centuries to make Kasuzuke (sake lees pickles; see page 110). Sake kasu can be purchased in slab or paste form at Japanese grocery stores (look for it in the fridge or freezer section). Note: Sake kasu contains a tiny bit of alcohol, from the sake-making process.

Kombu

Kombu comes in many forms, from large sheets to pre-cut pieces, and any type will work. Kombu is used to add umami to pickles, especially for quick pickles that don't involve fermentation. For Kombu jime (see page 242), larger sheets of kombu are easier to use.

When I walk along the beach, I collect washed-up seaweed, especially bull kelp, golden kelp and kombu. I put it out to dry in the sun and then use it in my cooking. Foraging can be done anytime, anywhere!

Chillies

In Japan, dried red chilli is used to discourage insects from long-fermenting pickles such as Nukazuke (see page 186) and Hakusai zuke (see page 254). I often forget to store dried chillies, so I end up using fresh red chillies. It still works! I also use chillies in some quick pickles, but not for spiciness; they help add a refined and balanced flavour to the pickles.

I always remove the seeds first as red chillies are quite hot for me.

Kiriboshi daikon (dried daikon)

This nutritious and fibre-rich preserved food is a common ingredient in Japanese home cooking. It is made by cutting daikon into thin strips and sun-drying it. It's easy to make at home – simply cut the daikon and let it dry in the sun. In pickling, kiriboshi daikon is often used to absorb excess moisture from the pickling bed.

Kori-dofu (dried tofu)

Dried tofu is a popular ingredient in both shōjin ryōri (Buddhist cuisine) and Japanese home cooking. It's a traditional preserved food made by utilising the environment during the cold winters in Japan. Sliced tofu is hung outside, where it repeatedly freezes and dries, creating a unique spongy texture. It absorbs broth and seasonings well. Like kiriboshi daikon, in pickling, kori-dofu is often used to absorb excess moisture from the pickling bed.

Sugar

Like salt, sugar helps prevent spoilage, enhances preservation and draws out moisture from vegetables through osmosis. But it also has a moisture-retaining effect, which gives the pickles a pleasant texture. Additionally, sugar adds depth to the end flavour, which is why many recipes include it. However, if you are not a fan of sweet flavours, you can try making pickles without sugar. To be honest, I often skip adding sugar myself, depending on my mood. Alternatively, if you find some of the recipes in this book not sweet enough, do not hesitate to add some more – simply adjust to your own liking.

I use raw sugar, rapadura sugar or muscovado sugar in my pickles. These three sugars add depth to the flavours. For a clean and clear sweetness, raw caster sugar is also a good choice. You can also use honey, maple syrup or agave syrup.

SALT
お塩

I use natural sea salt when making otsukemono, as it contains lots of natural minerals. If you have a favourite salt, try using it, or compare how different salts affect the flavour of your pickles. Because pickles are so simple, the quality of each ingredient matters. I don't recommend using table salt – refined salt contains more than 99.5 per cent sodium chloride and almost no minerals.

When I travel I often buy salt as a little souvenir. They all have different tastes, colours and crystal shapes. Quite interesting. I also make salt from seawater. It's fun to do and it's kind of a miracle to see seawater turn into crystallised salt.

Sea salt

This is my recipe for making sea salt from nothing but seawater. From 1 litre (34 fl oz) of seawater, you will get around 30 g (1 oz) of sea salt.

1. Collect seawater.
2. Using trays, sun-dry the seawater until it has reduced to 10 per cent of its original volume. Strain the seawater into a saucepan, then bring to the boil and cook for about 10 minutes, until it has reduced further and turned a whitish colour.
3. Remove the pan from the heat and pass the liquid through a coffee filter (or similar) into a clean bowl. The white residue left in the filter consists of gypsum from the seawater, so we will say goodbye to that, or use it in the garden.
4. Clean the pan, then add the filtered seawater and bring to the boil again. Reduce the heat to low and simmer until the liquid turns white and starts to crystallise. Try not to agitate or stir the seawater too much at this stage – this will result in bigger salt crystals. Remove from the heat while some moisture remains in the pan.
5. Using a ladle, filter the mixture again through a coffee filter into a bowl. The salt will remain in the filter, while the liquid collected in the bowl is called 'nigari'. This is what we use to make tofu!
6. Separate the salt crystals left in the filter and let them dry in the sun for 1–2 days (sun-dried sea salt!). Or you can dry-roast them in a frying pan over low heat for 10–15 minutes, until completely dry.

VINEGAR

お酢

Vinegar is often used in pickling to add acidity and enhance preservation. In Japan, rice vinegar and grain vinegar are the most popular and they're sold everywhere. I prefer rice vinegar (or brown rice vinegar), as it has a milder acidity compared to grain vinegar, with a subtle hint of sweetness from the rice (make sure the label says 'pure rice vinegar' (純米酢)). My favourite vinegar is Fujisu Premium, a very special vinegar by Iio Jozo. It has a gentle acidity, soft aroma and beautiful rich umami flavour.

When making otsukemono, I don't have strict rules on what sort of vinegar should be used. Where I live in Australia, apples and pears grow well and it's common to find these fruits left on doorsteps when they're in season, gifted by friends or neighbours when the harvest has yielded more than they can use. I also forage for fruits during my walks and bring some home. Of course, you can't eat them all at once, so I make fruit vinegar with them. Apple vinegar, pear vinegar and even persimmon vinegar are the ones I make. Therefore, I use these homemade vinegars to make my otsukemono. Fruit vinegars also add a fruitiness to the pickles, which I like. Making fruit vinegar is not difficult. If you want to have a go, here are my recipes for apple cider vinegar and persimmon vinegar.

Persimmon vinegar

FERMENTATION TIME: *1 month–several years*

You will need

persimmons (any variety)

You can use any type of persimmon to make persimmon vinegar: sweet, astringent, soft, unripe ... I get overripe persimmons from a farmer who sells persimmons at my local farmers' market. He gives me the ones that are too soft to sell.

The most important thing to remember when making persimmon vinegar is not to wash the persimmons. If you really have to, just wipe them lightly. Acetic acid bacteria and wild yeast live on the skin of the fruit, and we don't want to wash them off.

1. Remove any stalks from the persimmons and break the fruit apart to encourage fermentation. If the persimmons are fully ripe and soft, you can easily crush them by hand. For firmer ones, use a hammer or a similar tool to break them up. As you crush the persimmons into manageable pieces, pack them into a large clean jar. And that's it! Cover the jar with a clean tea towel and secure with an elastic band. You don't need a lid.
2. Place the jar in a cool place away from direct sunlight. The next day, you will notice small bubbles forming as the fermentation begins. Since any solids floating on top can lead to mold growth, stir the mixture every 2–3 days using a clean spoon or a spatula.
3. The persimmons undergo an alcoholic fermentation phase before gradually turning into vinegar. To check if the alcoholic fermentation is complete, look for no bubbles even after stirring. This typically happens after about 1 month.
4. Once the fermentation is complete, you need to separate the solids from the liquid. I find that straining the mixture twice works best. First strain the vinegar through a coarse sieve set over a clean bowl and leave it to strain overnight. The next day, strain the vinegar again, this time through muslin (cheesecloth) or a coffee filter. I also leave this overnight or for a day.
5. The liquid is persimmon vinegar! You can use it right away or allow it to mature further from a few months to a few years. The flavour and colour will vary significantly depending on how long the vinegar is fermented – some prefer a fresher, younger taste, while others enjoy the depth of matured vinegar.

STORAGE: *Keep the persimmon vinegar in a cool, dark place for 5–10 years.*

Apple cider vinegar

FERMENTATION: TIME *2–3 months*

You will need

5 small apples (about 500 g/1 lb 2 oz)

1.25 litres (42 fl oz) water

60 g (2 oz) sugar (optional)

50 ml (1¾ fl oz) apple cider vinegar

Even if you're not familiar with fermentation, apple cider vinegar is easy to make at home and much more cost-effective than buying store-bought varieties. I highly recommend making it yourself.

1. Chop the apples and add them to a 2 litre (68 fl oz) glass jar, including the skins and cores. I like to combine different varieties of apples, as there are so many near where we live.
2. Add the water, sugar and apple cider vinegar – I use vinegar from last year's batch. If this is your first year making vinegar, then use an unpasteurised store-bought apple cider vinegar.
3. Gently stir the mixture, then cover the jar with a clean tea towel, secured with an elastic band. We don't want any unwelcome insects inside! Keep the real lid nearby. For the first two weeks, gently shake the jar every day. Remove the tea towel, close with the lid and shake. Then take the lid off and put the tea towel back on, secured with the elastic band.
4. After a few days bubbles will start to develop – this is a good sign that fermentation has started. The apple will turn brown and the liquid will become cloudy.
5. After two weeks, the bubbling will subside and the liquid will become more cloudy. Strain the liquid through muslin (cheesecloth) or a fine-mesh sieve into a clean jar. (If you didn't add sugar, keep shaking the liquid daily for about 2 months, then strain.) You can use the strained apple in cooking! Puree it and use as a marinade or sauce.
6. Cover the jar with a tea towel and elastic band and leave the liquid to ferment, without shaking, for at least 3 months. After 3 months, taste the vinegar. If you like the flavour, you can bottle it. If you're not sure, use a Ph level checker to check the acidity. If the Ph level is 3–3.5, the vinegar is ready to bottle.

STORAGE: *Store the apple cider vinegar in a cool, dark place for up to 2 years.*

MY JAPANESE VEGETABLE GARDEN

日本の野菜を育てる

I like to grow vegetables (and fruits) in my garden. Even when I lived in a tiny apartment, I always grew things. Maybe it's because I watched Dad grow all the vegetables for the family when I was young – it's always seemed very natural to me.

Every day, I wake up before sunrise and go outside. Early mornings are such a special moment in the garden. The air is crisp and clean, the birds are singing around me or laughing (yes, kookaburra!), the vegetables look happy in the morning dew.

Since moving to Australia from Japan, growing vegetables has become even more important to me. It is not easy (or even possible) to source Japanese vegetables, especially after I moved to a small village in the countryside with a population of 1000 people. So now I focus on growing Japanese vegetables.

There are some challenges. The climate here is different from Japan. It's not cold enough for some vegetables to grow happily (daikon and other green leafy vegetables, for example), and they often send up their flower stalks too soon. The timing of the seasons can also be a problem. When my ume tree starts to blossom, it often coincides with heavy storms. Crazy rain, hail and strong winds blow away the flowers, making pollination difficult. The weather is also still cold and bees are not active yet! So I use my ear-cleaner pom-pom to help pollinate the flowers and hope that no storm comes.

The soil in my garden is also different from what I grew up with in Japan. I am constantly battling with slugs and snails. I want them to learn how to share food with me. But all challenges make good projects. I still enjoy the process – even if I fail, that's just part of nature, I may not get a crop that year, but I'll try again next year, and gradually learn what works and what doesn't.

JAPANESE VEGETABLES, HERBS & FRUITS I GROW IN MY GARDEN

I source the seeds and seedlings in Australia, often online, sometimes from friends. I am still looking for Japanese flavours to grow! Japanese sansho (pepper tree), udo (mountain asparagus), fuki ...

Vegetables:

– Daikon
– Japanese turnips
– Edamame (soybeans)
– Shungiku (edible chrysanthemum)
– Gobo (burdock)
– Satoimo (Japanese taro)
– Nagaimo (Japanese yam)
– Komatsuna, yukina, mizuna (leafy greens)
– Japanese cucumber
– Japanese eggplant (aubergine)
– Negi (Japanese spring onion/scallion)
– Rakkyo (Chinese allium)
– Shishito

Herbs:

– Shiso (ao jiso, green perilla; aka jiso, red perilla)
– Myoga (Japanese ginger flower buds)
– Mitsuba
– Wasabi

Fruits:

– Yuzu (Japanese citrus)
– Sudachi (Japanese citrus)
– Ume (Japanese plum/apricot)
– Nashi (kosui and hosui; Japanese pear)
– Kaki (persimmon)
– Mikan (Japanese mandarin)

And rice – it's so beautiful to grow rice! Many creatures love my rice paddy – to them, it's like an oasis.

AMAZU ZUKE

甘酢漬け

Amazu means 'sweet vinegar' in Japanese, and amazu zuke are simple pickles made with sweetened vinegar. You can easily and successfully pickle any vegetable and the results are delicious. It also preserves very well. It's a pickle with many benefits.

The flavour of your pickles will change depending on the type of vinegar you use – rice vinegar, grain vinegar, apple cider vinegar or persimmon vinegar. I often use homemade persimmon or apple cider vinegar (see pages 33 and 34), which gives a fruity taste. I also enjoy the flavour of rice vinegar. Feel free to experiment with whatever vinegar you have at home or your favourite type. Also, feel free to adjust the sweetness as you prefer.

For me, the charm of sweet-vinegar pickling is how the colours of the vegetables become vibrant. When pickling vegetables with red pigments, the colour change is especially striking. Additionally, white vegetables become an even brighter white because the vinegar prevents discolouration.

These pickles have excellent preservation qualities. The antibacterial effects of vinegar and the sterilising power of salt allow the pickles to be stored for extended periods.

Some of these pickles are made for specific purposes, like New Year's celebrations, while others are made with the seasonal harvest.

For those who might feel uncertain about the pickling process, sweet-vinegar pickling is a fail-safe method.

RED ONION AMAZU ZUKE

赤玉ねぎの甘酢漬け

PICKLING TIME: *3 days*

You will need
1 red onion

Pickling liquid
30 ml (1 fl oz) vinegar
5 g sugar
2 g salt

STORAGE: *Store in a clean jar in the refrigerator for up to 1 month.*

Onions are said to have many health benefits including blood-thinning properties when eaten raw. However, raw onions can be too sharp in taste for many. Try them pickled in sweet vinegar and you'll find them much easier to enjoy.

This pickled dish often makes an appearance at my family dinners from late summer through to autumn when we harvest red onions from the garden.

1. Peel the red onion, cut it into thin wedges and place in a bowl.
2. Combine the pickling ingredients in a bowl, mixing well until the sugar and salt have dissolved.
3. Pour the pickling liquid over the red onion.
4. Place a plate on top as a weight.
5. Allow the pickles to rest in the refrigerator for at least 3 days or until they become a nice red-pink colour.

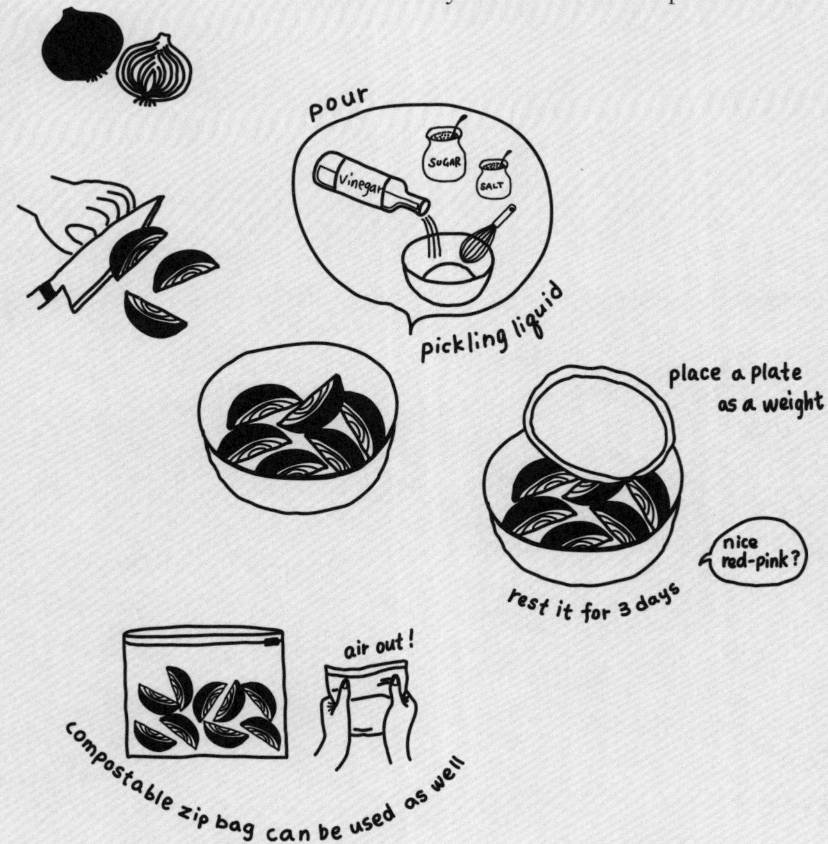

KOUHAKU NAMASU

紅白なます

PICKLING TIME: *30 minutes*

You will need
500 g (1 lb 2 oz) daikon
50 g (1 ¾ oz) carrot
1 yuzu or lemon (optional)
5 g salt
toasted sesame seeds, to serve

Pickling liquid
100 ml (3 ½ fl oz) vinegar
20–25 g (¾–1 oz) sugar
2 g salt
15 ml (½ fl oz) citrus juice such as yuzu, sudachi, orange or mandarin (optional)

STORAGE: *Store in the refrigerator for up to 10 days.*

Kouhaku means 'red and white' in Japanese, and this colour combination is often used for celebrations such as New Year, weddings, school graduations and births. This pickle is one of the most iconic celebratory dishes. The white of the daikon and the red of the carrot (if you can find red carrots use those instead of the usual orange ones) represent these festive colours. Sometimes I even add yellow carrots just for fun. I love it so much that I often make it throughout the year. It adds freshness and helps cleanse the palate during meals.

Daikon is rich in digestive enzymes that help break down carbohydrates, proteins and fats, so having this dish alongside a rich main course is a great way to support digestion. The flavour of daikon varies depending on which part of the root you use. The top part is sweeter, the middle has a pleasant texture and juiciness, while the lower part is more peppery. For this namasu, I usually avoid the lower part of the daikon and prefer the middle-to-top sections.

Namasu can also be made with other vegetables. In autumn, when fresh lotus root is available, I make lotus root namasu (see page 70). When I can find fresh persimmon, I add it to the kouhaku namasu as well. In winter, add some strips of yuzu peel to the mixture for an elegant, aromatic touch. You can even add sashimi – just cut it into strips or thin slices and mix it in. There are so many variations to explore!

1. Peel the daikon and carrot but don't throw the peels away – use them in other dishes like miso soup or kinpira.
2. Slice the daikon diagonally into 3–4 mm (⅛ in) slices, about 7–8 cm (2 ¾–3 ¼ in) long. Stack the slices, slightly offset, and cut them again into 3–4 mm (⅛ in) strips. This technique is called the namasu cut. By cutting across the fibres, the texture becomes more tender and the flavours blend beautifully.
3. Cut the carrot into thin strips in the same way as the daikon but a bit shorter – about 5–6 cm (2–2 ½ in) in length.
4. If using yuzu or lemon, peel a strip off the outer yellow part only. Don't include any pith as it is bitter. Finely slice the peel. (Use the rest for something else.)

CONTINUED →

5. Place the daikon and carrot in a colander or bowl and sprinkle them with the salt to draw out excess moisture. Mix well with your hands and leave to rest for 10 minutes while you prepare the pickling liquid.
6. Combine the pickling liquid ingredients in a bowl, mixing well until the sugar and salt have dissolved.
7. Using both hands, squeeze the liquid out of the daikon and carrot mixture thoroughly, then put them in a clean container. If you are using yuzu or lemon peel, add it now. Pour the pickling mixture over the vegetables and gently loosen them with chopsticks or a fork to ensure the flavours are evenly distributed.
8. Put a lid on the container and allow the pickles to rest in the refrigerator for at least 30 minutes, although overnight is preferable for the flavour to permeate throughout.
9. To serve, top with toasted sesame seeds.

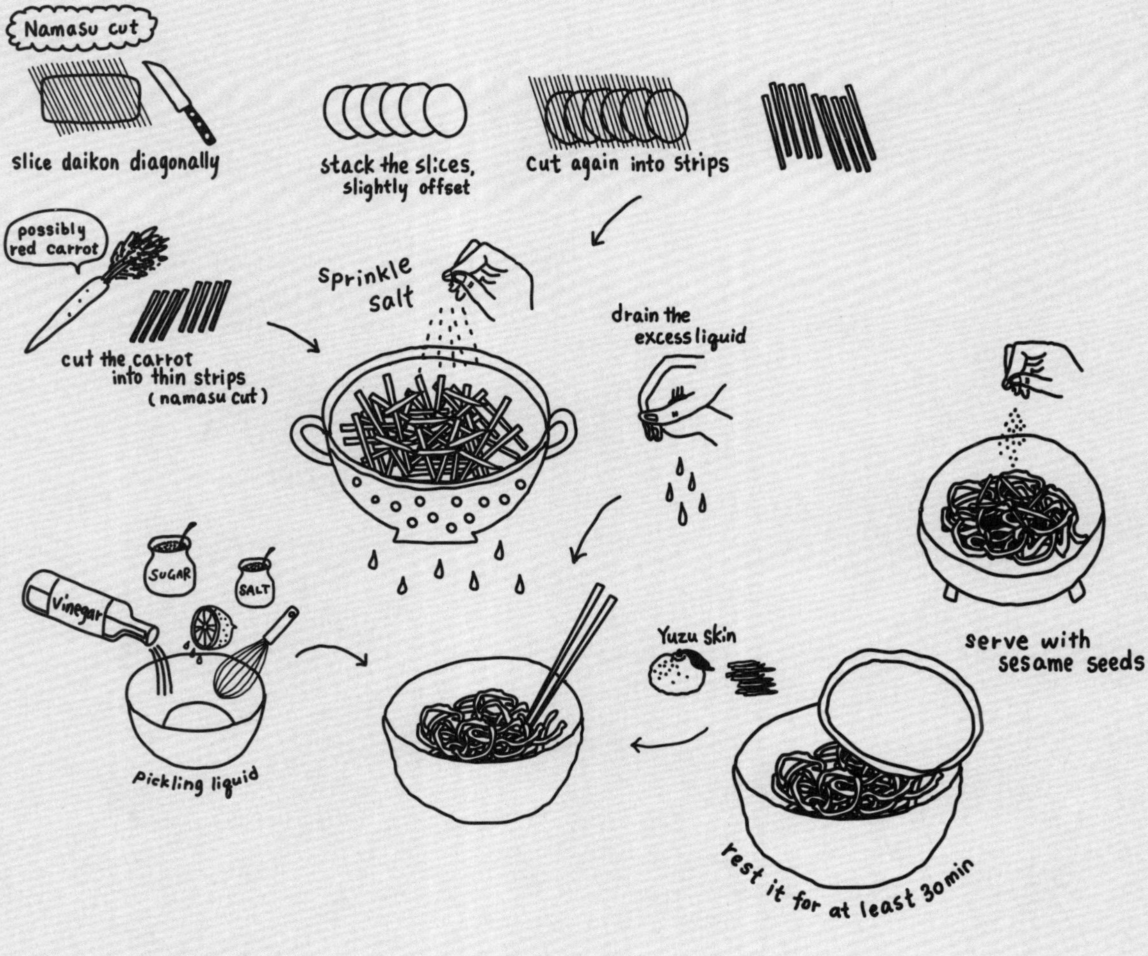

RED TURNIP AMAZU ZUKE

赤かぶの甘酢漬け

PICKLING TIME: *1 day*

You will need
300 g (10½ oz) red turnip
salt (2 % of turnip weight)

Pickling liquid
100 ml (3½ fl oz) vinegar
20–25 g (¾–1 oz) sugar
5 g salt

STORAGE: *Store in a clean jar in the refrigerator for up to 2 weeks.*

I have loved red turnips since I was little. The first time I tried red turnip pickles was at my relatives' house, and it was a sensational experience. I knew it was turnip, but the flavour was unlike anything I had ever tasted – there was something unique about it compared to regular white turnip. To my younger self, it tasted like an 'adult' flavour. Looking back now, I think that 'adult' taste came from the slightly bitter polyphenols. The vibrant, deep-red colour, almost a pinkish purple, fascinated me.

In Japan, we have more than 80 varieties of turnips, including many types of red turnips. Every time I see turnips at the market it brings back that sweet childhood memory and I can't resist buying them to make red turnip pickles.

1. Cut the top and bottom off the turnip, then cut it in half. Slice each half into wedges or 1–2 cm (½–¾ in) pieces.
2. Weigh the turnip pieces to calculate the amount of salt required in the next step.
3. Place the turnip pieces in a colander or bowl and sprinkle them with the salt to draw out excess moisture.
4. Allow the turnip pieces to rest for 10 minutes, or until you see they have released moisture.
5. Meanwhile, combine the pickling liquid ingredients in a bowl, mixing well until the sugar and salt have dissolved.
6. Drain the moisture off the turnip pieces, then add them to the pickling liquid. Place a plate on top as a weight.
7. Allow the pickles to rest in the refrigerator for at least 1 day before serving.

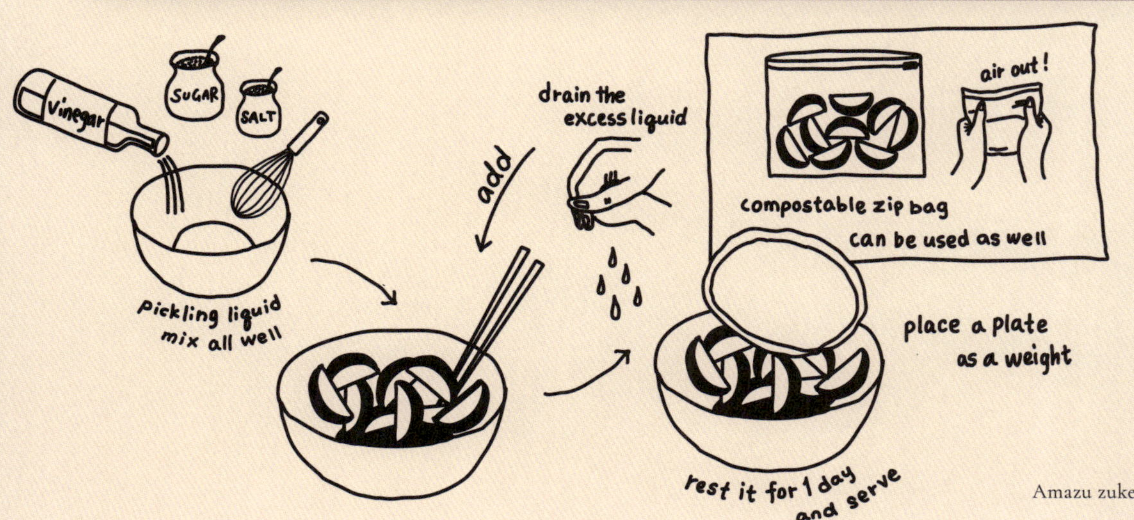

Vinegar
SUGAR
SALT
pickling liquid
mix all well
add
drain the
excess liquid
compostable zip bag
can be used as well
air out!
place a plate
as a weight
rest it for 1 day
and serve

GARI

ガリ

PICKLING TIME: *4–6 hours*

You will need
500 g (1 lb 2 oz) fresh young ginger

Pickling liquid
250 ml (8½ oz) vinegar
35–40 g (1¼–1½ oz) sugar
6 g salt

STORAGE: *Store in the refrigerator for up to 1 year.*

Yes, this is the pickled ginger you eat with sushi.

These are seasonal pickles that I only make when I can find fresh young ginger at the market. Finding the ginger is probably the most difficult part of making these pickles – but it's worth the effort.

The cute pink colour comes naturally from the pigment in the young ginger. When you make it yourself, it's not only delicious and refreshing, but you can enjoy it without additives or preservatives.

1. Prepare the pickling liquid by gently warming the vinegar, sugar and salt in a small saucepan while stirring over low heat until the sugar and salt have dissolved completely. Set aside while you prepare the ginger.
2. Wash the young ginger thoroughly using a brush. Peel away all the brown skin, if necessary. If the ginger is very fresh, there may not be much brown skin to remove.
3. Slice the ginger very thinly along the fibres. Very, very thin. If you have a mandoline that can create ultra-thin slices, feel free to use that. However, most mandolines can't slice that thin, so I prefer to use a knife. Enjoy the mindfulness moment!
4. Soak the sliced ginger in a bowl of water for 10–15 minutes.
5. Bring a saucepan of water to the boil, then add the sliced ginger. The cooking time will depend on your taste preference: for a spicier ginger kick, cook for only 30 seconds; for a milder flavour, cook for 3 minutes. (You can use this ginger cooking liquid in a drink. Enjoy it with chai, ginger ale, cola ...)
6. Remove the ginger from the pan and place the pieces on a zaru (flat bamboo basket) or in a colander.
7. While it is still warm, use both hands to squeeze the water out of the ginger, then put it in a clean jar. Immediately pour the pickling liquid into the jar so that it covers the ginger completely.
8. Once it has cooled, seal the jar and allow the pickles to rest in the refrigerator for 4–6 hours before serving.

Squeeze
the water out

Cute
gentle
pink
colour
yum!

ROLLED YUZU DAIKON AMAZU ZUKE

ゆず巻き大根

PICKLING TIME: *2 days*

You will need

500 g (1 lb 2 oz) daikon
3–4 yuzu

Pickling liquid option 1

100 ml (3½ fl oz) vinegar (or add some yuzu juice from the yuzu to make it 100 ml/3½ fl oz total)
25 g (¾ oz) sugar
3 g salt

Pickling liquid option 2

40 ml (1¼ fl oz) soy sauce
40 ml (1¼ fl oz) vinegar
40 ml (1¼ fl oz) mirin

STORAGE: *Store in the refrigerator for up to 1 month.*

— *NOTE:* Dried rolled yuzu daikon is famous in the region where I grew up. If you'd like to try this, thread a needle and pierce the rolled daikon pieces, stacking them on top of each other. Hang the rolled daikon in a well-ventilated place for 1–2 weeks to dry. Hanging the rolled daikon will help preserve it. It is also very pretty. You can then use the dried daikon to make the pickles.

This is also one of my favourite pickles (I know, I have many favourite pickles) and, more than anything, it makes me happy in terms of its form, colour and, of course, its flavour. Although the flavour is the same as the yuzu daikon on page 68 (as it uses the same ingredients), this one excites me so much more because it's rolled! And yuzu is hiding inside!

Whenever I find these pickles in the refrigerator at my parents' house I do a little dance. After I left my parents' house and started to make this for my family and friends, I realised how many steps are involved – these rolled yuzu daikon are full of love.

To make the daikon rollable, it needs to be sun-dried. I enjoy seeing sliced daikon sun-bathing in my garden. It's very peaceful. I place my flat baskets of daikon on the washing rack on nice, sunny, cold days.

I have included two options for pickling the rolled daikon. Option 1 is a sweet vinegar that retains the beautiful white colour of the daikon. Option 2, known colloquially as '3 cups vinegar', uses soy sauce, which will produce a brownish colour pickle. I had this version at my friend's house and it was yummy.

1. Cut the daikon into 2 mm (1/16 in) slices. Place the slices on a zaru (flat bamboo basket), or similar, and put them out to dry in the sun for up to a day, until they become floppy and can be rolled up.
2. Peel the yuzu skin, but don't include any pith as it is bitter. Finely slice the peel into strips, hopefully the width of the daikon slices. If the strips are too short, you can overlap a few pieces to achieve the desired length.
3. Place a few strips of yuzu on a slice of dried daikon and roll it up tightly. (You can dry them again at this stage – see Note – but it's not necessary.)
4. Place the daikon – rolled ends down to prevent them from opening – in a container with a lid. If you have excess sliced daikon or yuzu peel, put it on top of the rolled daikon.
5. Choose the pickling liquid you want to try. For option 1, simply combine the ingredients in a jar and mix well. For option 2, bring the ingredients to the boil in a small saucepan, then set aside to cool.
6. Pour the pickling liquid on top of the rolled daikon and pop on the lid.
7. Allow the pickles to rest in the refrigerator for at least 2 days before serving.

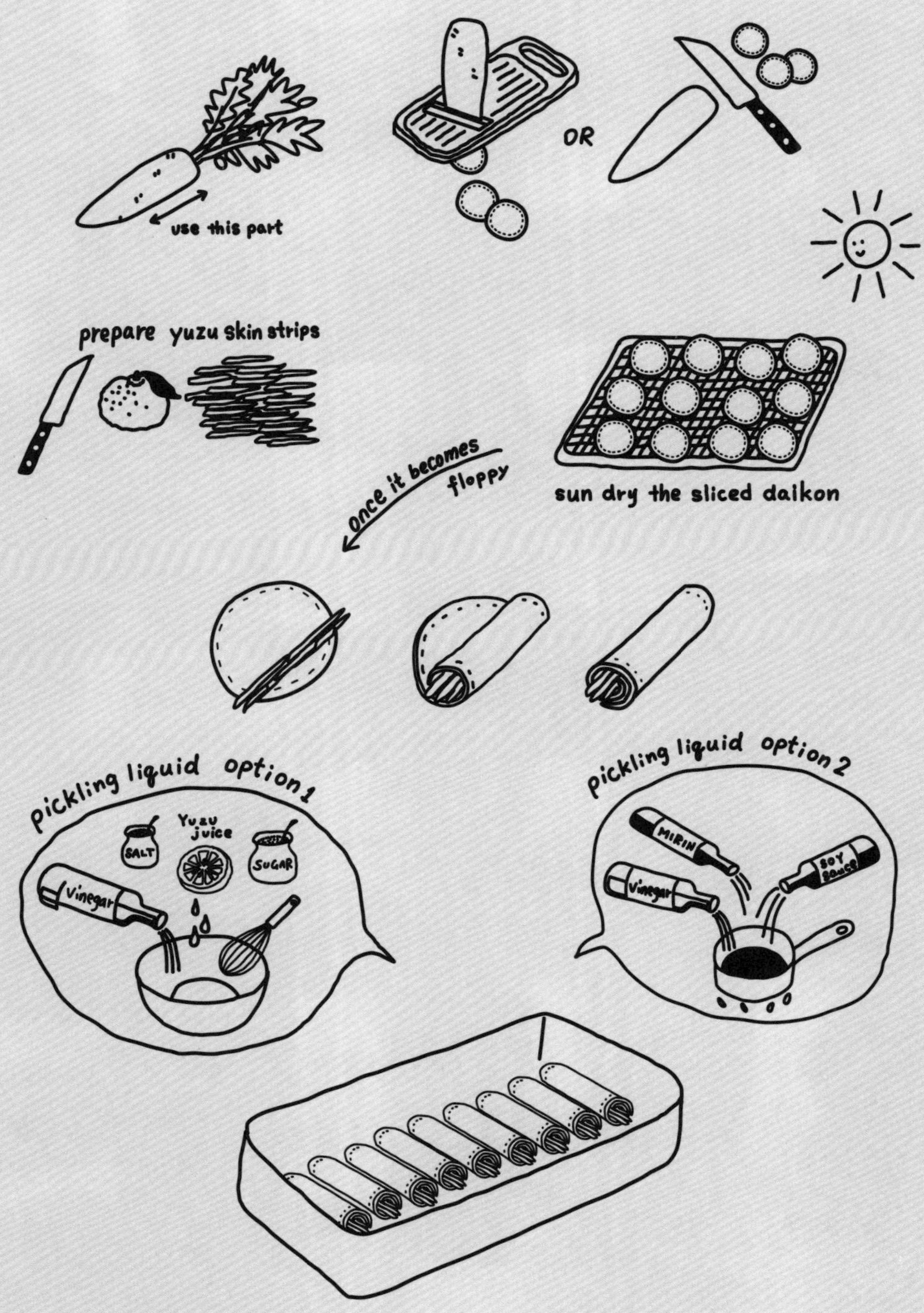
use this part
OR
prepare yuzu skin strips
sun dry the sliced daikon
once it becomes floppy
pickling liquid option 1
SALT
Yuzu juice
SUGAR
Vinegar
pickling liquid option 2
MIRIN
SOY SAUCE
Vinegar

PINK RADISH AMAZU ZUKE

二十日大根の甘酢漬け

PICKLING TIME: *3 days*

You will need
150 g (5½ oz) red radishes
4 g sugar (2–3 % of radish weight without leaves)
60 ml (2 fl oz) vinegar

STORAGE: *Store in the refrigerator for up to 1 month.*

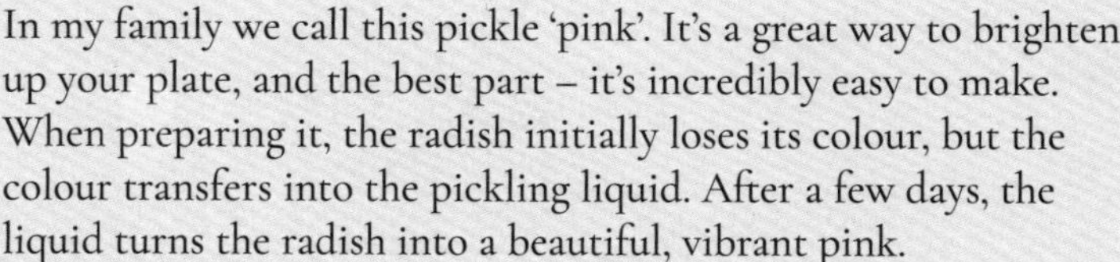

In my family we call this pickle 'pink'. It's a great way to brighten up your plate, and the best part – it's incredibly easy to make. When preparing it, the radish initially loses its colour, but the colour transfers into the pickling liquid. After a few days, the liquid turns the radish into a beautiful, vibrant pink.

I find the colour is perfect by the third day. You can keep it longer if you want but, interestingly, if you leave it too long the radish colour fades again. Where does the colour go, I wonder?

This pickle uses the natural 'water' from the radish itself, so we don't need to use much vinegar.

1. Cut the radish leaves off but don't throw them away – use them in other dishes. If the radishes are large, cut them into bite-sized pieces. If they're small, you can leave them whole. Depending on the size, I sometimes halve or quarter them.
2. Weigh the radishes to calculate the amount of sugar required.
3. Place the radishes in a clean jar. Sprinkle the sugar over the top, pop the lid on and shake the jar to evenly distribute the sugar.
4. Take the lid off and add the vinegar. Pop the lid back on tightly and turn the jar upside down and leave it in the refrigerator overnight.
5. The next day, return the jar to its original upright position so that the top radishes can now soak in the pickling liquid. You can flip the jar upside down as much as you like, or shake it – all of the radishes will be pickled after 3 days.

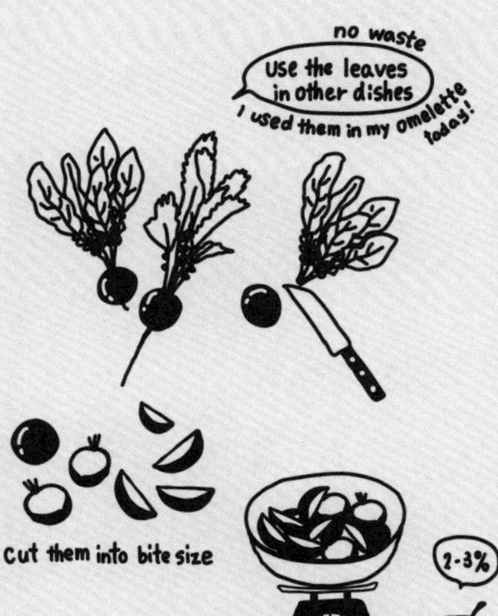

CHRYSANTHEMUM TURNIP AMAZU ZUKE

菊花かぶ

PICKLING TIME: *30 minutes*

You will need

300 g (10½ oz) small turnips
salted water (3 % salt)
1 yuzu or lemon
½ small red chilli

Pickling liquid

100 ml (3½ fl oz) vinegar
15 g (½ oz) sugar
3 g salt

STORAGE: *Store in a clean container in the refrigerator for up to 10 days.*

This famous cutting technique, known as *kikka kabu* in Japan, turns turnips into pretty chrysanthemum flowers. Like kouhaku namasu (see page 48), this pickle is also served at celebratory occasions.

I make this pickle for when I have people over or as part of a degustation meal. Just by scoring the turnips and placing a ring of chilli or yuzu strips in the middle, they become pretty flowers. It is actually a lot simpler than it looks. By using different coloured turnips or radishes, you can create many variations. Score thinly or thickly, make short or long petals ... enjoy the creative process.

1. Cut the top and bottom off the turnips. These parts won't bloom into flowers but you can still use them to make pickles or add them to miso soup, salads or any other dishes, so don't throw them away. Use a sharp knife to score the turnips, leaving 5 mm (¼ in) from the bottom intact. I put a pair of chopsticks on either side of the turnip, so that I can avoid accidentally cutting through to the bottom. Rotate the turnip 90 degrees, then cut again in the same way.
2. Soak the turnips in the salted water for 30 minutes at room temperature, until the petal parts become floppy.
3. Meanwhile, slice a strip of yuzu peel off the outer yellow part only. Don't include any pith as it is bitter. Thinly slice the strip of peel. Remove the seeds from the chilli and slice it into thin rings.
4. To make the pickling liquid, combine the pickling ingredients in a bowl, mixing well until the sugar and salt have dissolved.
5. Remove the turnips from the water. Using both hands, squeeze the water out of the turnips, then place them in a small bowl.
6. Pour the pickling liquid on top and add a plate as a weight.
7. Allow the turnips to rest at room temperature for 30 minutes.
8. Remove the turnips from the pickling liquid and gently prise open the petal sections to form a flower shape.
9. To create the flower centre, you can place a small amount of yellow yuzu peel in the middle of the chrysanthemum and top it with a red chilli ring if you like. There are no rules; this is the creative part.

— *NOTE:* I prefer to use small turnips because it's easier to make a reasonably sized flower. If you use a big turnip, cut it in half or quarters.

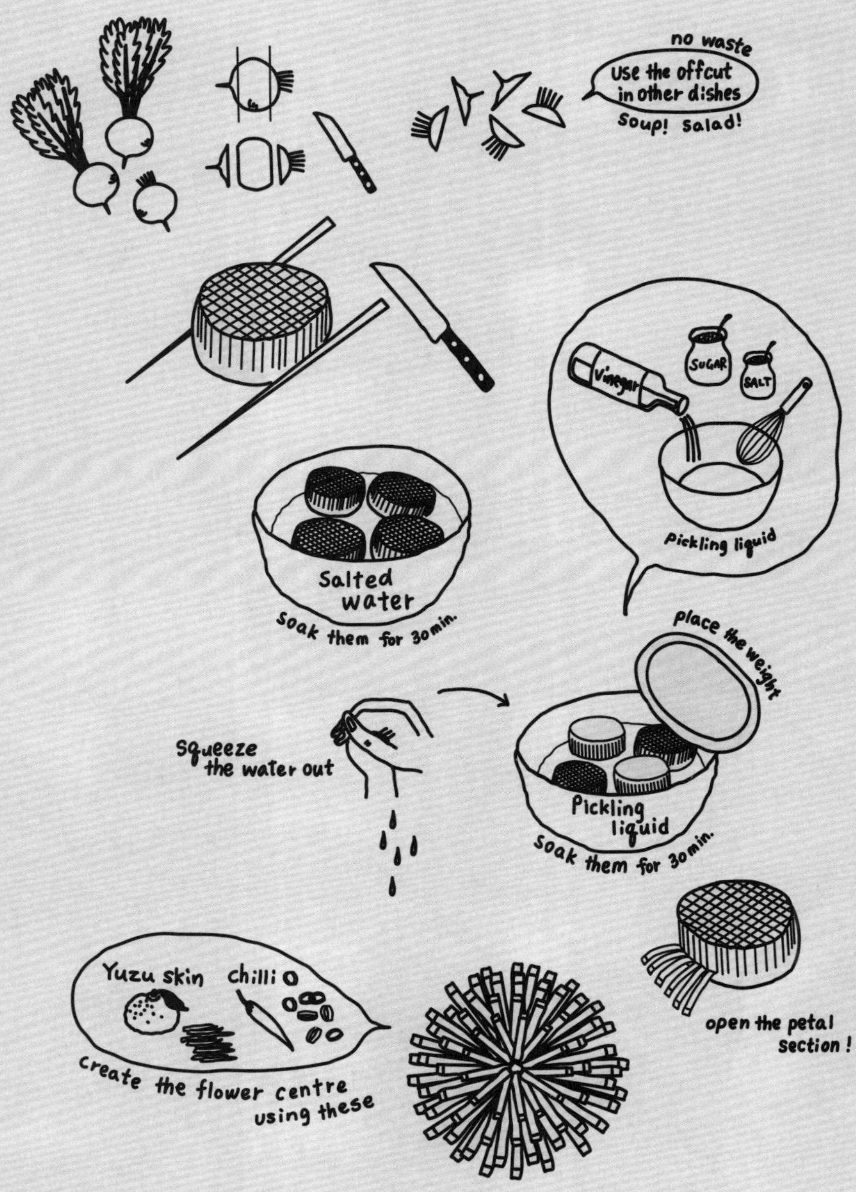
no waste
Use the offcut in other dishes
Soup! Salad!
Vinegar
SUGAR
SALT
Pickling liquid
Salted water
Soak them for 30min.
place the weight
Squeeze the water out
Pickling liquid
Soak them for 30min.
Yuzu skin
chilli
create the flower centre using these
open the petal section!

YUZU DAIKON AMAZU ZUKE

ゆず大根

PICKLING TIME: *1 hour*

You will need
500 g (1 lb 2 oz) daikon (for this pickle, I normally use the top part)
15 g salt (3 % of daikon weight)
1 yuzu

Pickling liquid
60 ml (2 fl oz) vinegar
juice of 1 yuzu
20 g (¾ oz) sugar
pinch of salt

STORAGE: *Store in a clean container in the refrigerator for up to 1 week.*

This simple yet delicious pickle is one of my favourites, making winter something to eagerly anticipate. Aroma plays a crucial role in pickling, and the addition of yuzu in this pickle elevates the flavours, making the dish even more delightful.

At my family home we have a large yuzu tree that produces an abundance of fruits: we use the green yuzu at the end of autumn and the bright-yellow ones throughout winter in various dishes. With such a plentiful supply, we even make yuzu jam and put many yuzu into the bathtub (yuzu bath!). We also grow plenty of daikon, which often features in our meals and pickles. The way you cut and prepare daikon can transform its texture, making it an incredibly versatile vegetable. Although daikon is available year-round, winter daikon is particularly special: it's tender, juicy and sweet. Using this delicious winter daikon to make yuzu pickles creates a truly exceptional dish.

1. Cut the daikon into 1 cm × 4 cm (½ in × 1½ in) matchsticks.
2. Place the daikon pieces in a colander or bowl and sprinkle them with the salt to draw out excess moisture. Place a plate on top as a weight and allow the daikon to rest for 10–15 minutes.
3. Meanwhile, slice a strip or two of yuzu peel off the outer yellow part. Don't include any pith as it is bitter. Finely slice the peel.
4. To make the pickling liquid, combine the ingredients in a bowl, mixing well until the sugar and salt have dissolved.
5. Using both hands, squeeze the water out of the daikon, then place it in a clean container or bowl with the yuzu peel. Pour the pickling liquid on top and place a plate on top as a weight.
6. Allow the pickles to rest in the refrigerator for at least 1 hour before serving.

— *NOTES:* If yuzu is too bitter for your taste, you can blanch it briefly before adding it to the pickling liquid.

If you peel the daikon you will get a cleaner finish. I personally don't peel any vegetable skins when I cook for my family, but I sometimes peel them when I have guests.

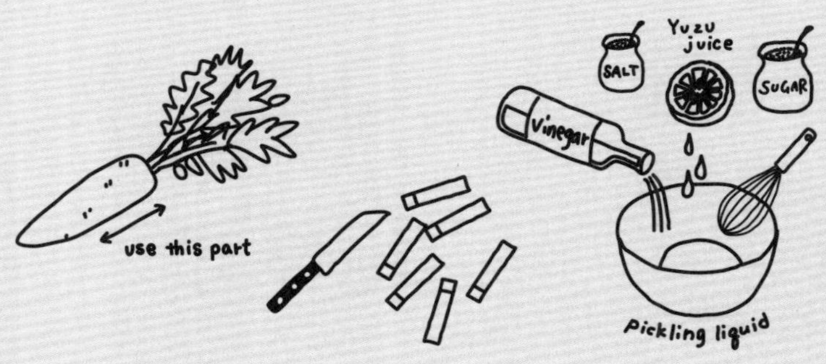

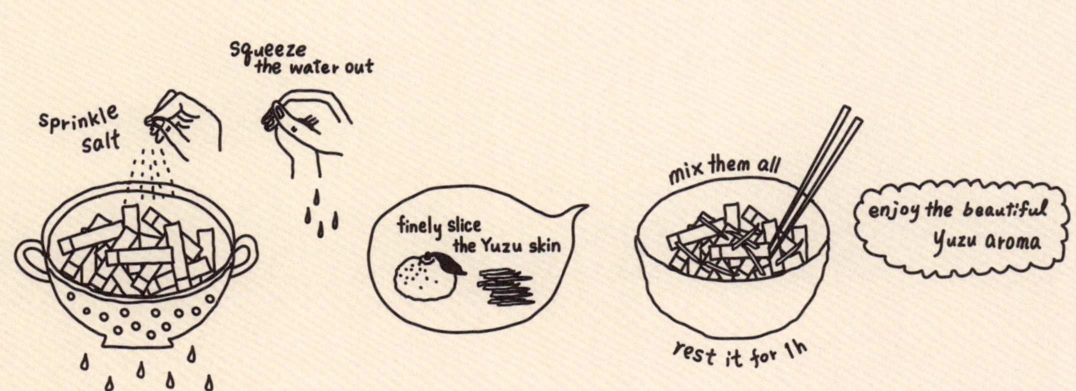
Squeeze the water out
Sprinkle salt
finely slice the Yuzu skin
mix them all
rest it for 1h
enjoy the beautiful Yuzu aroma

LOTUS ROOT AMAZU ZUKE

れんこんの甘酢漬け

PICKLING TIME: *30 minutes*

You will need

15–20 cm (6–8 in) section of fresh lotus root

¼ dried red chilli (optional)

15 ml (½ fl oz) yuzu or lemon juice

Pickling liquid

80 ml (2 ¾ fl oz) vinegar

20 g (¾ oz) sugar

3 g salt

STORAGE: *Store in the refrigerator for up to 10 days.*

Lotus root is such a pretty vegetable. I even collect goods that have lotus root designs on them. We call this vegetable renkon. I like the sound of it, too. This vegetable is considered an auspicious food in Japan because the holes symbolise a clear view of the future. They are used in New Year's dishes and for other celebrations to welcome good prospects.

The texture of lotus root is truly unique; we describe its crunchiness as *shaki shaki*. This delightful crispness adds an enjoyable contrast to various dishes. Fresh lotus roots are typically available in Asian grocery stores during their peak season, which runs from autumn through to winter. Although lotus roots are available frozen, they often lose their unique texture in the freezing process. For this pickle, I highly recommend finding fresh lotus root to ensure the best flavour and crunch.

This pickle can be used as a sushi ingredient, and it adds a nice texture to sushi rice. It's also a great garnish with fish or teriyaki chicken. It's also a beautiful little dish just by itself.

1. Peel the lotus root and finely slice it into rings. Place the slices in a bowl of water to prevent discolouration.
2. If using, remove the seeds from the chilli and finely slice it into rings.
3. Bring the pickling liquid ingredients to the boil in a small saucepan, then add the sliced lotus root and cook for 1 minute, ensuring it retains its crispness.
4. Remove the pan from the heat and allow the mixture to cool.
5. Once cool, add the citrus juice for a touch of brightness. Add the chilli for a touch of heat, if desired.
6. Transfer the pickles and pickling liquid to a clean container and allow them to rest in the refrigerator for at least 30 minutes before serving.

— *NOTE:* If you cut around the edge of the lotus root it will look like a flower. I use this cut for special occasions.

Cook for 1 min.
Cool off
optional
chilli
Yuzu juice
pickle them for at least 30 min

ASAZUKE

浅漬け

Asazuke are quick, simple pickles made with seasonal vegetables. The 'asa' in asazuke refers to the short pickling time. It allows you to fully appreciate the freshness of the vegetables. You can either rub the vegetables with salt or soak them in a light pickling liquid, creating a dish that's enjoyed much like a salad. Although they have a salad-like feel, most asazuke use no oil at all, making them incredibly healthy and easier to eat than raw vegetables. Adding small amounts of seasonings, such as ginger or shiso, gives them a refreshing flavour, and the variations are endless. Asazuke magically enhance the vegetables' vibrant colours, which make them even more appealing.

Asazuke are quick and easy to prepare and incredibly satisfying. They are the perfect way to enjoy seasonal produce, which is why I believe they're the most commonly made pickle in modern households. In my home, we make them in every season except winter. You can quickly prepare asazuke while making dinner, and they're ready with the perfect flavour and texture by the time you're sitting down to eat. Asazuke are ideal both as a snack and a palate cleanser, hence their popularity on izakaya menus.

CELERY ASAZUKE

セロリの浅漬け

PICKLING TIME: *10 minutes*

You will need
200 g (7 oz) celery stalks
½ red chilli

Pickling liquid
5–10 g sugar
30 ml (1 fl oz) vinegar
5 cm (2 in) square of dried kombu, cut into thin strips
5 g salt

STORAGE: *Store in a clean container in the refrigerator for up to 10 days.*

Celery pickles hold a special place in my heart. Although celery is not a traditional Japanese vegetable, I was pleasantly surprised to discover how delicious it can be when pickled in the Japanese style. In Japan, celery asazuke is sold at quite high prices in department store basements, and I always hesitated to purchase it. However, since moving to Australia, where celery is readily available, I've started making this pickled dish more frequently.

The thing I love about this celery asazuke is definitely texture. The crunch of celery while you're eating makes this asazuke very fun. It's asazuke, so of course it makes the most of the celery's freshness. The beautiful fresh green celery with a hint of red chilli makes a great contrast on your plate. The chilli I use here is not really for hotness – at least for me (I can't handle spicy food very well), but it does add a tiny kick and enhances the beautiful celery flavour.

Serve these pickles as a palate cleanser when you serve rich food. I like to pair this pickle with cute pink radish otsukemono (see page 63).

1. Carefully remove the hard strings from the celery, then diagonally cut the stalks into 1–1.5 cm (½ in) slices. Remove the seeds from the chilli and finely slice it into rings.
2. Combine the celery, chilli, sugar, vinegar, kombu and salt in a bowl.
3. Use your fingers to gently massage the celery for 1–2 minutes, until you feel moisture begin to release.
4. Place a plate on top of the celery as a weight.
5. Allow the celery to rest in the refrigerator for at least 10 minutes before serving, but the next day it's even better. You can enjoy it like a salad for the first day, and from the second day onwards, the flavours deepen, making it even more delicious!

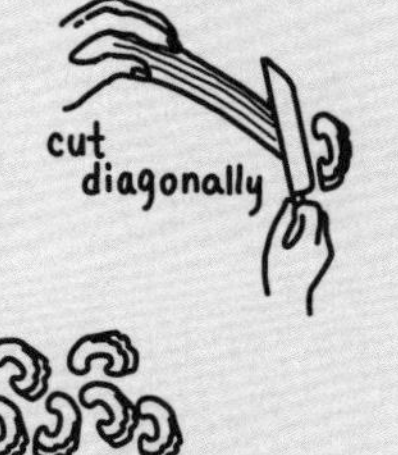

CUCUMBER & GINGER ASAZUKE

きゅうりと千切り生姜の浅漬け

PICKLING TIME: *10 minutes*

You will need

2–3 thin cucumbers
10–15 g ginger
salt (2 % of cucumber weight)
soy sauce, to serve (optional)

STORAGE: *Store in a clean container in the refrigerator for up to 2 days.*

I used to make this pickle often when I was a student working at a soba kappo–style restaurant. In kappo dining, the chef prepares and cooks right in front of the customers over the counter (fancy!) … while lots of behind-the-scenes prep takes place backstage. In the restaurant where I worked the mother-in-law of the chef helped out in the back kitchen and I often worked alongside her. She was sweet and kind (a grandmother to me) and, like the chef, she also showed me many techniques and shared her knowledge with me. At the restaurant we always served soba or rice dishes with a small plate of quick pickles. This cucumber and ginger asazuke was the one we most often made. I remember massaging the vegetables alongside this lovely grandmother.

1. Slice the cucumbers into 1 cm (½ in) rounds. Finely julienne the ginger.
2. Weigh the cucumber to calculate the amount of salt required in the next step.
3. Combine the cucumber and ginger in a bowl, add the salt, then use your fingers to gently massage the vegetables for 1–2 minutes.
4. Place a plate on top of the vegetables as a weight.
5. Allow the pickles to rest for at least 10 minutes before you eat them.
6. Serve and enjoy. I love eating this as is, but you can also add a dash of soy sauce. We call this *ajihen*, meaning 'flavour change'!

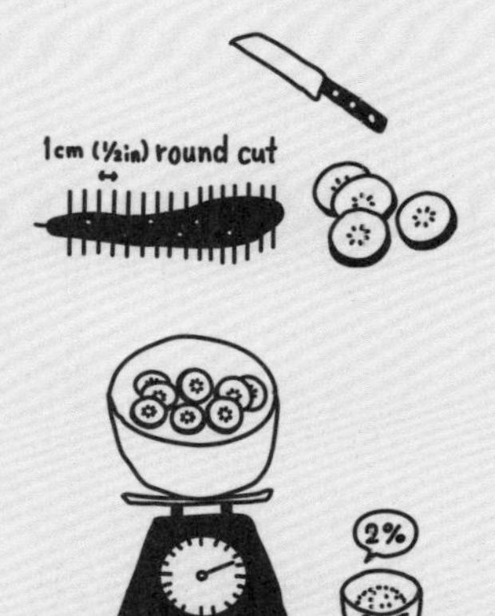

TURNIP & TURNIP LEAF ASAZUKE

蕪と蕪の葉の浅漬け

PICKLING TIME: *30 minutes*

You will need

3 small turnips with leaves (preferably the Japanese hakurei variety)

salt (3 % of turnip weight)

5 cm (2 in) square of dried kombu, cut into thin strips (optional)

10 g sugar dissolved in 30 ml (1 fl oz) vinegar (optional)

STORAGE: *Store in a clean container in the refrigerator for up to 5 days.*

Turnips are a fantastic vegetable for pickling. They have a natural sweetness and a wonderful balance of softness and firmness – truly perfect. I often find the Japanese variety, specifically the small white hakurei turnip, at farmers' markets. Hakurei are excellent both raw in salads and for pickles.

Whenever we didn't have pickles ready for dinner, my mum would say, 'Oh no, we're out of pickles,' and swiftly prepare this asazuke as part of the meal. I've always loved the vibrant colour contrast between the bright-white turnip and its vivid green leaves and, of course, the flavour combination.

If you find the leaves a bit bitter or strong in flavour, try adding a little vinegar and sugar – this will make them easier to enjoy. To enhance the umami and deepen the flavour, add some kombu.

1. Cut the top 1 cm (½ in) off the turnips, retaining the leaves. Wash around the leaf stems thoroughly, using a thin stick (like a toothpick) to ensure there's no residual sand or dirt. Put the leaves aside.
2. Slice the turnips lengthways into halves, then slice them again lengthways into 3–4 mm (⅛ in) pieces. Cut the thicker leaf stems (the part attached to the turnips) into 2 cm (¾ in) pieces for extra colour. I don't use the rest of the leaves for this pickle, but I often make another dish from them; for example, furikake (a Japanese condiment sprinkled over rice or noodles; see page 80).
3. Weigh the turnip to calculate the amount of salt required in the next step.
4. Combine the turnip, chopped stems and kombu (if using) in a bowl. Add the salt, then use your fingers to gently massage the turnip and stems for 1–2 minutes. Now is the time to add the sugar and vinegar solution if you are using it.
5. Place a plate on top as a weight.
6. Allow the pickles to rest in the refrigerator for at least 30 minutes before serving. If you have the time, a day is ideal to achieve the best flavour.

— *NOTE:* Small turnips weighing around 100 g (3 ½ oz) each are recommended for asazuke so you don't need to peel the skin.

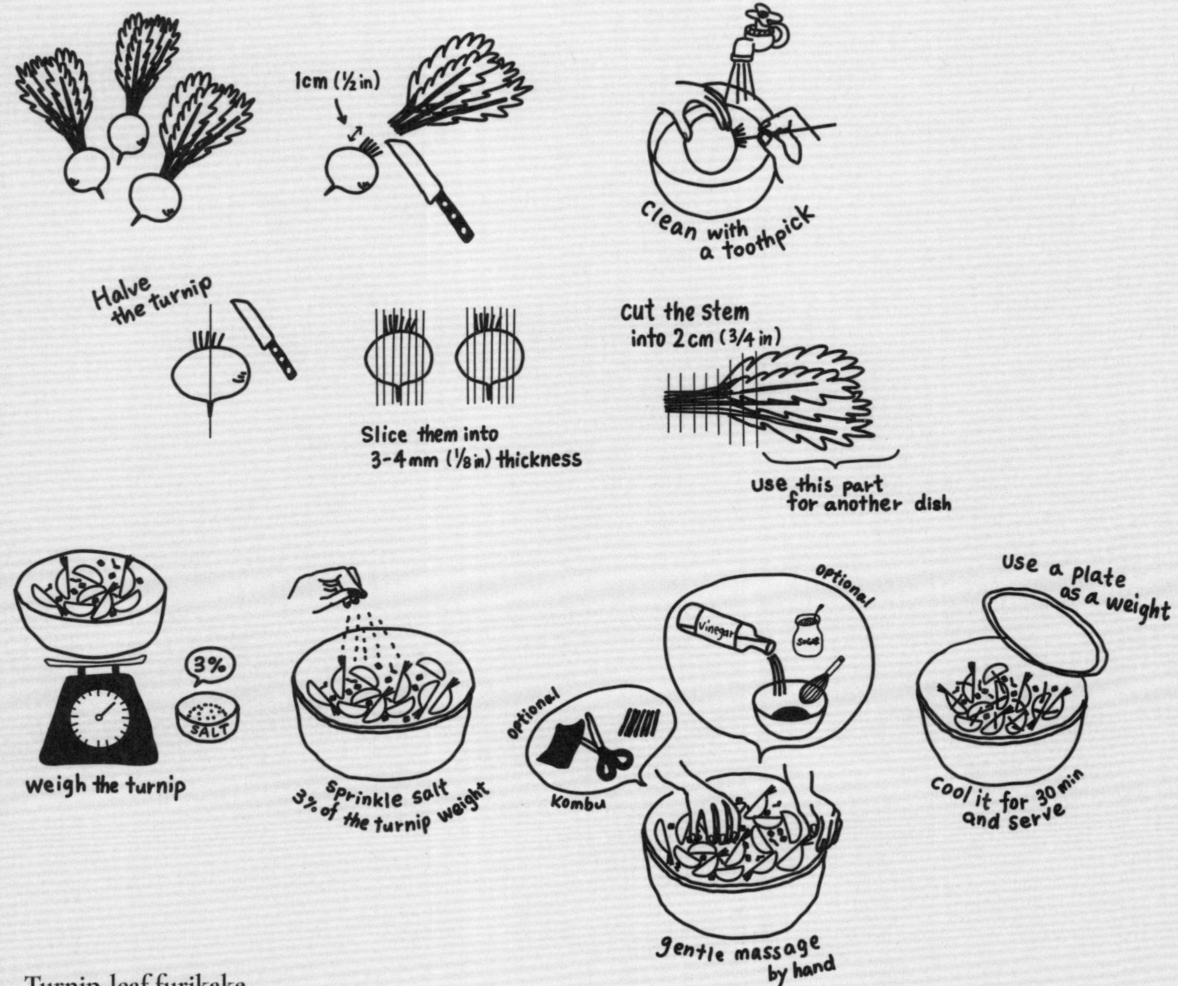

Turnip-leaf furikake

蕪の葉のふりかけ

Furikake can be made with mixed ingredients like dried seaweed, toasted sesame seeds, chopped green vegetables, such as the leaves of daikon or radish, and/or fish flakes. In winter, these vegetables grow in my garden and I often make furikake using the leaves.

To make furikake with turnip leaves, wash the leaves from three small turnips thoroughly and cut them into 5 mm (¼ in) pieces. Heat 15 ml (½ fl oz) of sesame oil in a frying pan over medium heat and stir-fry the leaves until they begin to soften, around 2–3 minutes. Add 30 ml (1 fl oz) of soy sauce, 15 ml (½ fl oz) of sake and 15 ml (½ fl oz) of mirin and simmer until the liquid has evaporated. Take it off the heat and mix in as many toasted sesame seeds as you like and it's ready to serve. Adding bonito flakes also makes it delicious. The furikake will keep in the refrigerator for 3–4 days.

CUCUMBER & GREEN SHISO LEAF ASAZUKE

きゅうりと青紫蘇の浅漬け

PICKLING TIME: *30 minutes*

You will need

as many thin cucumbers as you like
salt (2 % of cucumber weight)
green shiso leaves (1 leaf per cucumber used)
pinch of toasted sesame seeds

STORAGE: *Store in a clean container in the refrigerator for up to 2 days.*

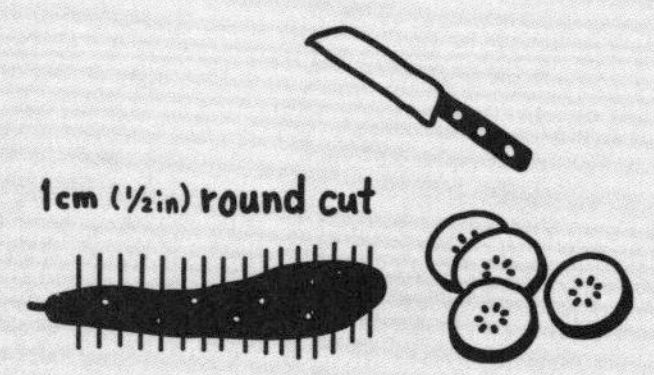

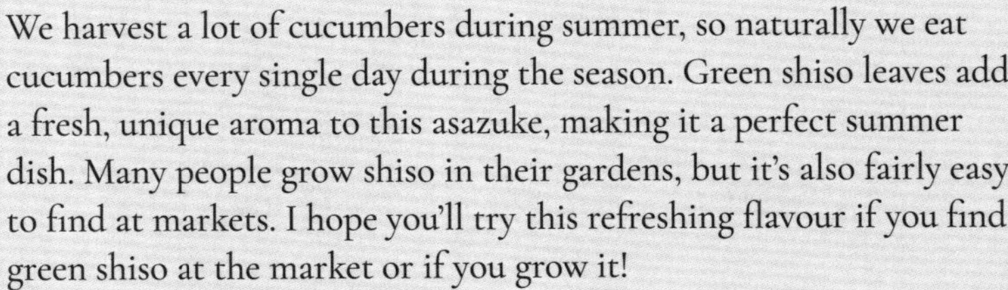

We harvest a lot of cucumbers during summer, so naturally we eat cucumbers every single day during the season. Green shiso leaves add a fresh, unique aroma to this asazuke, making it a perfect summer dish. Many people grow shiso in their gardens, but it's also fairly easy to find at markets. I hope you'll try this refreshing flavour if you find green shiso at the market or if you grow it!

1. Diagonally slice the cucumbers into 1 cm (½ in) rounds.
2. Weigh the cucumber pieces to calculate the amount of salt required in the next step.
3. Combine the cucumbers and salt in a bowl, then use your fingers to gently massage the cucumbers for 1–2 minutes. Set aside for 10 minutes, until the cucumber slices release their liquid.
4. Finely slice the green shiso leaves into 1–2 mm strips. If the leaves are large, cut them in half before slicing.
5. Drain the excess liquid off the cucumbers, then add the shiso leaves to the bowl and mix thoroughly.
6. Place a plate on top as a weight and allow the pickles to rest in the refrigerator for 30 minutes before serving.
7. Serve the pickles with hineri goma toasted sesame seeds. *Hineri goma* means to pinch the sesame seeds between your thumb and fingers as you sprinkle them, which releases their wonderful aroma.

CUCUMBER, TURNIP & MYOGA ASAZUKE

きゅうりと蕪とみょうがの浅漬け

PICKLING TIME: *30 minutes*

You will need
2 thin cucumbers
2 small turnips
salt (2 % of cucumber and turnip weight)
2–3 myoga (Japanese ginger flower buds)
15 g (½ oz) ginger
10 ml sesame oil
toasted sesame seeds, to serve (optional)

STORAGE: *Store in a clean container in the refrigerator for up to 2 days.*

Myoga, Japanese ginger flower buds, have a beautiful, distinctive aroma that evokes the seasons. Although myoga is not a common herb outside of Japan, I've noticed it becoming more available at nurseries recently, so it seems many people are growing it in their gardens. Despite being called Japanese ginger, we don't use the roots like regular ginger. Instead, we harvest the flower buds, which are about the size of a thumb. The buds are harvested from early summer ('summer myoga') to autumn ('autumn myoga').

Ideally, the buds are picked before they bloom. However, since the buds are nearly buried underground (just peeking out), it's a bit like treasure hunting. It reminds me of mushroom foraging – I kneel on the ground, scanning the surface for the tiny tips of the buds poking through. When I spot one, I dig around it with my fingers and uncover the lovely, chubby flower buds. It's such a joy!

Compared to the previous cucumber asazuke recipe, this version has a more mature flavour. The unique aroma of myoga combined with the richness of sesame oil stimulates the appetite.

Myoga is quite easy to grow, so why not give it a try for a unique addition to your kitchen garden?

1. Cut the cucumber into the rangiri shape (see page 24) or bite-sized pieces. Cut the leaves from the turnips, leaving 1 cm (½ in) of the stalk attached. Wash around the stalks thoroughly, using a thin stick (like a toothpick) to ensure there's no residual sand or dirt. Use the leaves in another dish. Cut the turnips into small wedges.
2. Weigh the cucumber and turnip pieces to calculate the amount of salt required in the next step.
3. Combine the cucumber, turnip and salt in a bowl, then use your fingers to gently massage the vegetables for 1–2 minutes. Set aside for 10 minutes or until the cucumber releases its moisture.
4. Meanwhile, cut the myoga in half lengthways then finely slice them. Finely julienne the ginger.
5. Drain any excess liquid from the cucumber and turnip, then add the myoga and ginger to the bowl. Add the sesame oil and mix well.
6. Place a plate on top as a weight.
7. Allow the pickles to rest in the refrigerator for 10 minutes.
8. If desired, sprinkle toasted sesame seeds on top of the pickles when serving for added flavour.

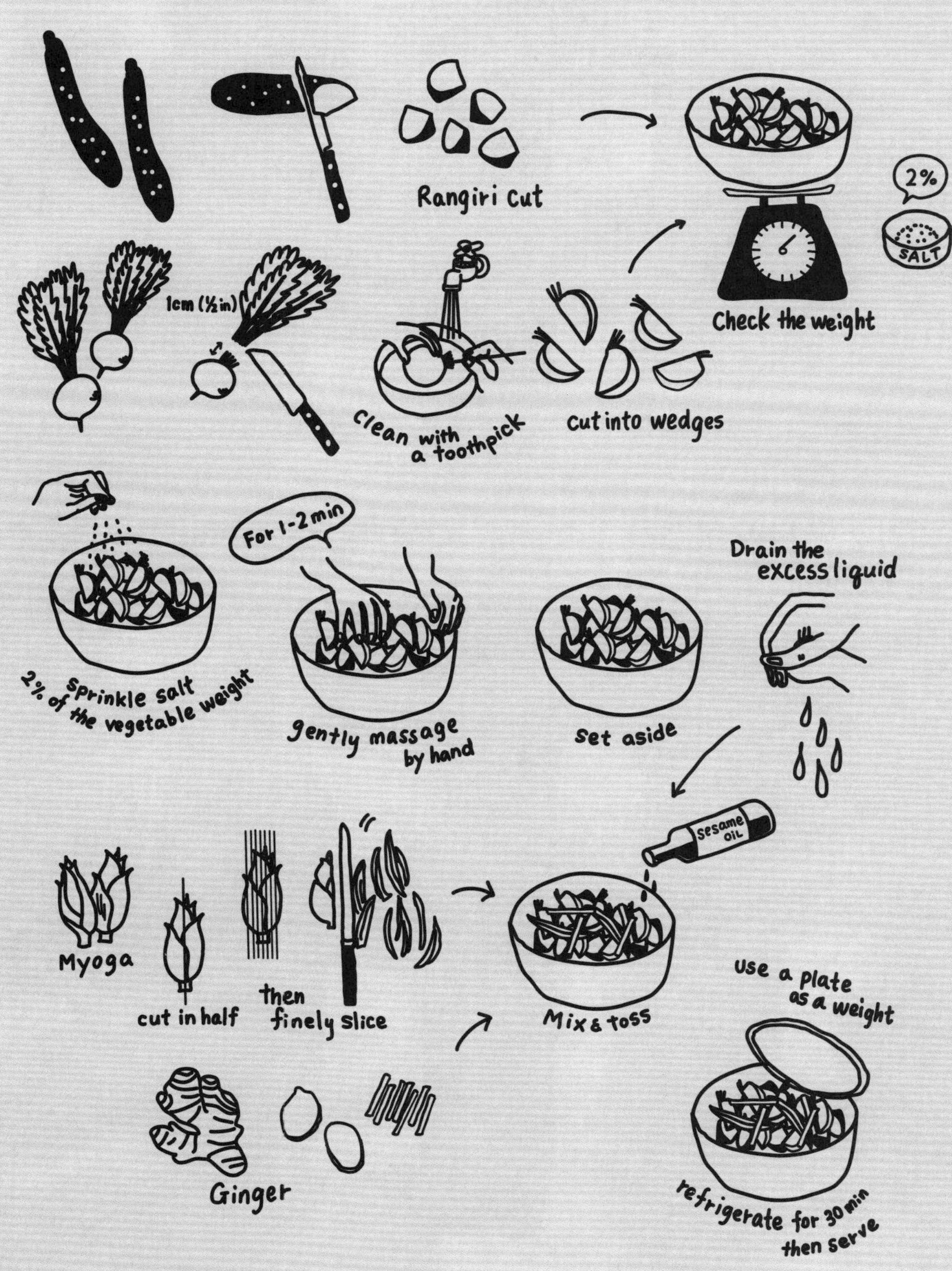
Rangiri cut
2%
SALT
Check the weight
1cm (½in)
Clean with a toothpick
Cut into wedges
For 1-2 min
Drain the excess liquid
Sprinkle salt 2% of the vegetable weight
gently massage by hand
set aside
Sesame OIL
Myoga
cut in half
then finely slice
Mix & toss
Use a plate as a weight
Ginger
refrigerate for 30 min then serve

CUCUMBER & UMEBOSHI ASAZUKE

うめきゅう

PICKLING TIME: *15 minutes*

You will need

2 thin cucumbers
sugar (1.5 % of cucumber weight)
2 unsweetened umeboshi
bonito flakes, to serve (optional)

STORAGE: *Store in a clean container in the refrigerator for up to 2 days.*

Here's another quick and easy cucumber pickle that I absolutely want to share. The combination of cucumber and umeboshi is simply wonderful. It's the perfect pickled dish to enjoy on a hot summer's day with the delightful flavour of umeboshi. While authentic, traditional umeboshi (without added flavours) is ideal, you can also use flavoured umeboshi – what I like to call 'modern umeboshi'. In that case, use salt instead of sugar in the recipe.

To prepare the cucumbers, we often hit them (sorry, cucumbers!) to create a textured surface instead of slicing them neatly with a knife. For this recipe, I even break them into smaller pieces by hand. Let's embrace the hands-on approach – it's fun and delicious, don't you think?

As for the umeboshi seeds, after you've removed the flesh of the fruit, pop one in your mouth. Umeboshi seeds have a candy-like quality (but not sweet at all). Suck on the seed to extract the salty umami flavour inside (trust me, there's more flavour to discover!).

1. Weigh the cucumbers to calculate how much sugar you will need.
2. Hit the cucumbers with something to make rough surface. I use a wooden stick called a surikogi (Japanese pestle), which is normally used with a suribachi (Japanese mortar) for grinding or mushing. You could use anything, like a rolling pin or a mug to squash them a bit. Tear the cucumbers into bite-sized pieces.
3. Put the cucumber pieces in a bowl. Add the sugar, then use your fingers to gently massage the cucumber for 1–2 minutes, until you feel moisture begin to release.
4. Tear the umeboshi flesh off the seed and chop it into small pieces.
5. Drain any excess liquid from the cucumber, then add the umeboshi.
6. Mix the umeboshi and cucumber well and allow it to rest for 15 minutes.
7. Serve with some bonito flakes if you like. Ume and bonito flakes are a great combination.

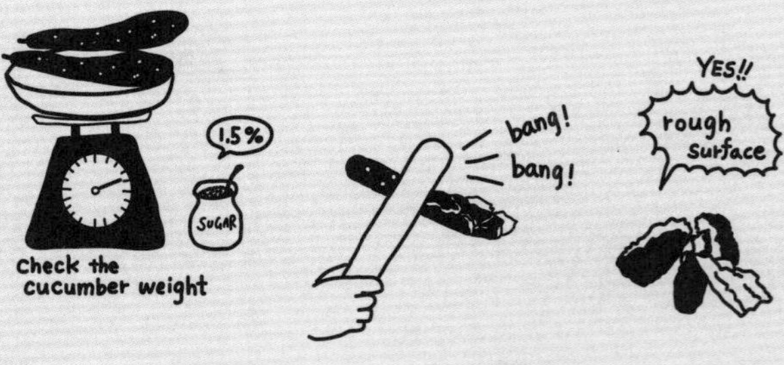

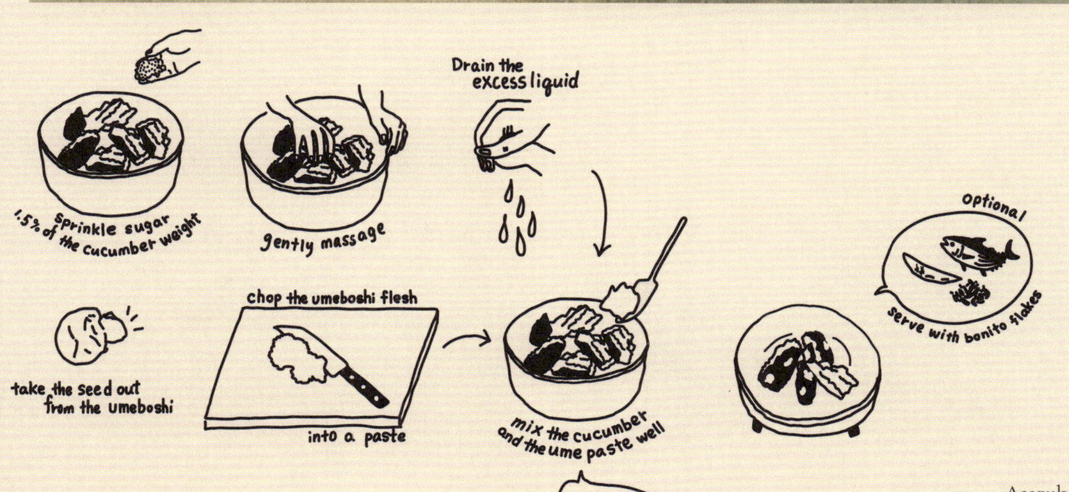
Sprinkle sugar
1.5% of the cucumber weight
gently massage
Drain the excess liquid
Optional
serve with bonito flakes
take the seed out from the umeboshi
chop the umeboshi flesh
into a paste
mix the cucumber and the ume paste well
Rest for 15min

SPRING CABBAGE, CARROT & GINGER ASAZUKE

春キャベツとにんじんの浅漬け

PICKLING TIME: *1 hour*

You will need
¼ spring cabbage
½ carrot
salt (2% of vegetable weight)
15 g (½ oz) ginger
5 cm (2 in) square of dried kombu, cut into thin strips (optional)

STORAGE: *Store in a clean container in the refrigerator for up to 1 week.*

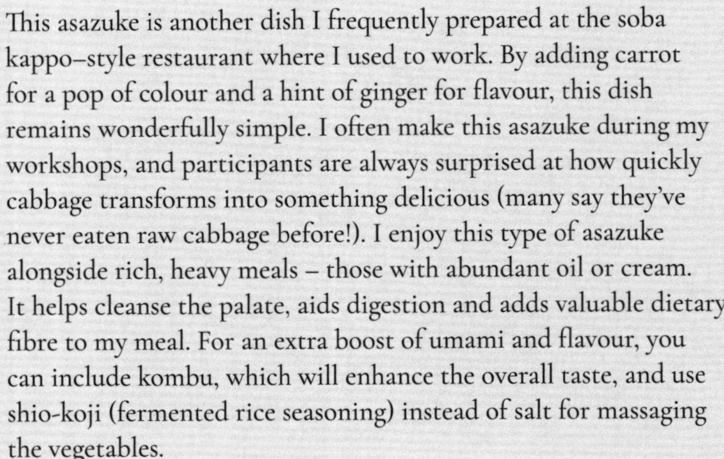

This asazuke is another dish I frequently prepared at the soba kappo–style restaurant where I used to work. By adding carrot for a pop of colour and a hint of ginger for flavour, this dish remains wonderfully simple. I often make this asazuke during my workshops, and participants are always surprised at how quickly cabbage transforms into something delicious (many say they've never eaten raw cabbage before!). I enjoy this type of asazuke alongside rich, heavy meals – those with abundant oil or cream. It helps cleanse the palate, aids digestion and adds valuable dietary fibre to my meal. For an extra boost of umami and flavour, you can include kombu, which will enhance the overall taste, and use shio-koji (fermented rice seasoning) instead of salt for massaging the vegetables.

1. First, weigh the cabbage and carrot to calculate how much salt you will need.
2. Cut or tear the cabbage into small, bite-sized pieces. (Spring cabbage is soft, so you can easily tear it.) Very finely slice the carrot into matchsticks. Finely slice the ginger into matchsticks.
3. Place the vegetables and kombu (if using) in a bowl, then add the salt. Use your hand to gently massage the vegetables (just like kneading dough) for 1–2 minutes.
4. Place a plate on top as a weight.
5. Allow the pickles to rest in the refrigerator for at least 1 hour before serving.

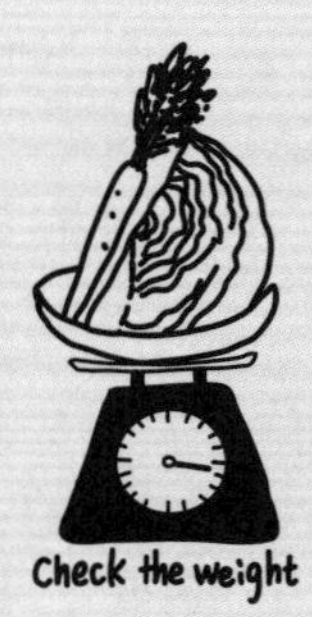

EGGPLANT ASAZUKE

なすの浅漬け

PICKLING TIME: *5 minutes*

You will need

2–3 small eggplants (aubergines)

6 g salt

finely sliced spring onion (scallion), myoga (Japanese ginger flower buds) or green shiso leaves, to serve (optional)

toasted sesame seeds and/or bonito flakes, to serve (optional)

Pickling liquid

5 ml soy sauce

5 ml vinegar

a few drops of sesame oil (optional)

This is one of the quintessential pickles of summer. Eggplants are a unique addition to pickles due to their spongy texture, which absorbs the pickling liquid and creates a deliciously flavourful bite. While eggplant is often cooked with oil, eggplant pickling offers a refreshing alternative. It's best to choose small, thin-skinned varietes for pickling, as they are consumed raw. Since eggplant tends to discolour after cutting, I recommend preparing this pickle at the very end of your meal prep and enjoying it right away, as it is not suitable for storing.

1. Cut the stalks off the eggplants, then slice the eggplant into thin wedges or cut them into bite-sized pieces and transfer to a bowl.
2. Sprinkle the salt evenly over the eggplant pieces, then press down firmly with your weight as you massage the eggplant, squeezing and kneading it for 1–2 minutes. As you do this the eggplant will gradually soften and become translucent. Once this happens, use your hands to squeeze out the excess moisture.
3. Place the squeezed eggplant back into the bowl and season it with the pickling liquid. Mix it through to combine the flavours.
4. Serve as is or incorporate some finely sliced herbs like spring onion, myoga or green shiso leaves to enhance the texture and make it a refreshing summer dish. You can also sprinkle some sesame seeds and/or bonito flakes for added flavour, if you like.

TURNIP & PERSIMMON ASAZUKE

蕪と柿の浅漬け

PICKLING TIME: *2 minutes*

You will need
2–3 small turnips
½ sweet persimmon (non-astringent)
pinch of salt
5 ml vinegar (optional)

STORAGE: *Store in a clean container in the refrigerator for up to 2 days.*

In my family's home we have a persimmon tree that produces delicious persimmons, both astringent and sweet, and when I was growing up I looked forward to enjoying the fruits every autumn. I've never tasted a persimmon that rivals its flavour and texture. The fun part is that you can't tell whether it's sweet or astringent until you peel it.

Despite being a wonderfully delicious variety – it is called the king of persimmons – these persimmons aren't available in markets because of the mix of sweet and astringent types – it's too risky to sell. Growing up alongside this tree, I developed a love for persimmons. This quick pickle pairs them with my other favourite ingredient: turnips. I believe firm, crispy persimmons are the best choice for this pickling recipe.

1. Cut the leaves off each turnip – use them in other dishes like miso soup or kinpira – leaving 1 cm (½ in) of the stalk attached. Wash around the stalks thoroughly, using a thin stick (like a toothpick) to ensure there's no residual sand or dirt.
2. Slice the turnips in half lengthways, then cut them into thin slices or wedges.
3. Cut the persimmon into pieces the same size as the turnip pieces. If you prefer, you can peel the persimmon (I usually leave the skin on).
4. Place the turnip and persimmon in a bowl, add the salt, then use your fingers to gently combine the pieces.
5. This mix is delicious as is, but if you feel it could use a touch more acidity, add some vinegar, to taste.

BENISHOGA

紅生姜

PICKLING TIME: *1 day*

You will need

300 g (10½ oz) young ginger (you can also use regular ginger)

9 g salt (3% of ginger)

Pickling liquid

100 ml (3½ fl oz) red umezu

100 ml (3½ fl oz) vinegar

STORAGE: *Store in the refrigerator for up to 6 months (or 1 year if you double-pickle; see page 98).*

— *NOTE*: The salt concentration of the red umezu can sometimes become too much. If this happens, add a little more vinegar. Taste it, and if you'd like a milder flavour, you can add 5 g sugar as an option.

The term *benishoga* literally means 'red ginger', and its refreshing flavour makes it a handy condiment to have in the refrigerator for various meals. Benishoga is often used as a topping for yakisoba (fried noodles) and okonomiyaki. It can also be found in round takoyaki (octopus balls) and makes a popular addition to tempura.

Store-bought versions often have a striking red colour due to the use of food colouring, but making benishoga at home means you can achieve a beautiful colour without relying on synthetic dyes. By using red umezu, either store-bought or homemade (a byproduct of making umeboshi; see page 273), you can create a vibrant pickle that's both visually appealing and healthy.

1. Wash the ginger thoroughly using a brush and peel any brown skin, if necessary. If the ginger is very fresh, there may not be much brown skin to remove.
2. Combine the whole ginger and salt in a clean container and place a 450–600 g (1–1 lb 5 oz) weight on top.
3. Allow it to rest for 1 day to draw out the moisture. Use a clean cloth or paper towel to wipe all the moisture off the ginger. At this stage you can slice the ginger into strips or leave it whole, depending on your preference.
4. Place the ginger on a zaru (flat bamboo basket) or in a colander and allow it to sun dry outside for 2–4 hours, until the surface of the ginger is lightly dry but not crinkly.
5. Transfer the ginger to a clean jar.
6. Combine the red umezu and vinegar, then pour the pickling liquid into the jar, ensuring the ginger is completely covered.
7. Allow the ginger to rest in the refrigerator for at least 1 day before eating. It will absorb the flavours of the liquid and develop a delicious taste.

Double-pickling your benishoga for longer preservation

長期保存するなら2度漬けがおすすめ

After about a week, discard the umezu and remove the ginger. Dry the ginger on a zaru again in the shade for 3–4 hours. Then place the ginger back in a clean jar and re-pickle it with a new mixture of umezu and vinegar to enhance its preservation. Treat the first pickling as the pre-pickling and the second pickling as the main pickling. If you want to make a large batch for long-term storage, double-pickling is recommended.

QUICK DAIKON UMEZU ZUKE

大根の梅酢浅漬け

PICKLING TIME *30 seconds*

You will need:

10 cm (4 in) length of daikon

5 ml red umezu

pinch of toasted sesame seeds using the hineri goma method (see page 82)

STORAGE: *Store in a clean container in the refrigerator for up to 2 days.*

Daikon is perhaps the most popular vegetable in Japanese cooking. It is used in a variety of ways – it can be added to salads, miso soup, simmered with fish, grated into daikon oroshi or pickled. Because of its versatility, many households have daikon in their refrigerators year-round. Thus, it often becomes a saviour when you find yourself saying, 'Oh no. I don't have any pickles!' Just chop up some daikon and mix it with red umezu and you have a delicious instant pickle. When my mother made pickles with daikon and red umezu, she would always sprinkle some toasted sesame seeds on top. The harmony of the plum and sesame aroma is truly appetising.

If you have Japanese herbs like shiso leaves or myoga (Japanese ginger flower buds) on hand, chop them up and mix them with the daikon for an even more refreshing pickle.

1. Finely slice the daikon into rounds, then cut the rounds into half-moons or quarters, depending on the size of your daikon.
2. Place the daikon slices in a bowl and add the red umezu. Use your fingers to gently massage the daikon with the umezu for 30 seconds, or until all the daikon slices turn a pretty pink colour.
3. Serve the pickles topped with toasted hineri goma sesame seeds.

— *NOTE*: The salt content of umezu will vary depending on how it's made. For example, umezu from my mum's umeboshi is a reduced-salt version, while store-bought ones will likely contain higher salt levels. Therefore, when using umezu in cooking, it's important to add it gradually and adjust the flavour as you go.

BEER ZUKE

ビールの一夜漬け

Beer pickles? Sounds fun! These recipes feature quick pickles made with beer as the pickling liquid. You can also try using apple cider or pear cider instead of beer. Luckily, I live in a region known for its apples and pears, so many local ciders can be found easily. Try different brands. Depending on what you use, the pickle flavour will change, so you can experiment with different flavours. Using beer allows you to create a deeply flavoured pickle in a short amount of time. A variety of vegetables work well with beer pickles – daikon and carrots are delicious choices, or you can enjoy summer vegetables such as bitter melon, zucchini (courgette) and bell peppers (capsicum). They all take on the flavour beautifully.

I'm not great with alcohol – except for sake, for some reason – so I make beer zuke with non-alcoholic beer. Of course, feel free to use any beer you have.

These pickles are perfect with rice or served as a side to meat or fish. You can pop them in burgers and sandwiches, or serve them with pies and pasties. They're also a great stand-alone dish. Yet, perhaps because of the name, I can't help but imagine an izakaya when I make these pickles. The lively atmosphere of people chatting over beer comes to mind so vividly. Because of this, I enjoy beer-pickled vegetables with izakaya food – like karaage and edamame. At my house, every Friday is izakaya night and these pickles are a great addition to the meal.

CUCUMBER & GARLIC BEER ZUKE

きゅうりとにんにくのビール漬け

PICKLING TIME: *overnight*

You will need
500 g (1 lb 2 oz) thin cucumbers
⅓ dried red chilli
1 garlic clove (if you have Garlic tamarizuke, see page 216, even better!)
10 green shiso leaves
5 cm (2 in) square of dried kombu

Pickling liquid
60 ml (2 fl oz) beer
30 ml (1 fl oz) vinegar
25 g (1 oz) sugar
20 g (¾ oz) salt

STORAGE: *Store in the refrigerator for up to 4 days.*

Cucumber paired with the kick of chilli and garlic works very well in this pickle. I also add shiso leaves and kombu – you can wrap the cucumber inside the pickled shiso leaves or place pickled shiso leaves on top of cheese and crackers, adding the cucumber and garlic on top, and serving as tapas.

You will probably find the texture of the kombu a bit slimy. Don't panic! It's normal. It's a type of water-soluble dietary fibre, and it helps reduce the absorption of sugars and fats. It's good stuff.

1. Slice the cucumbers accordion-style to ensure a deep flavour infusion. To do this, place a chopstick alongside the length of the cucumber, to avoid cutting through to the bottom. Remove the seeds from the chilli and finely slice it into rings. Finely slice the garlic.
2. Place the vegetables, shiso leaves and kombu in a compostable ziplock bag.
3. Combine the pickling ingredients in a bowl, mixing well until the sugar and salt have dissolved.
4. Pour the pickling liquid into the ziplock bag, press out as much air as possible and seal it closed.
5. Allow the pickles to rest overnight in the refrigerator.

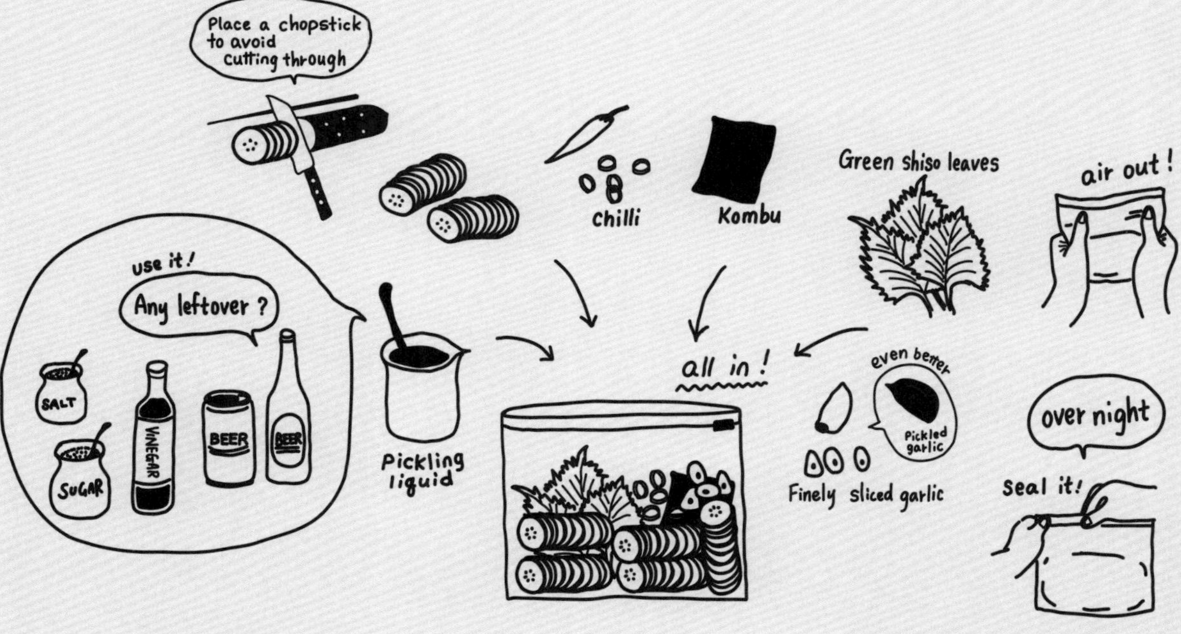

HAKUSAI BEER ZUKE

白菜のビール漬け

PICKLING TIME: *overnight*

You will need

1 kg (2 lb 3 oz) wombok (Chinese cabbage)

1 small red chilli

Pickling liquid

100 ml (3½ fl oz) beer

50 ml (1¾ fl oz) vinegar

80 g (2¾ oz) sugar

30 g (1 oz) salt

STORAGE: *Store these pickles in their liquid in a clean container in the refrigerator for up to 1 week.*

In Japan, when people gather for festivals or community events, beer and sake are often served. The beer comes in a big bottle like a wine bottle and is poured into individual glasses. Pouring alcohol in this way is part of Japan's communication style, I think. In Australia people tend to drink beer directly from small individual bottles. I find a glimpse of individualism even in things like this, which makes me feel the cultural differences. When people gather in Japan, many large bottles are provided on the table, but often some bottles have beer left over. Leftover beer! Since those beer bottles haven't been directly drunk from, you can use the leftovers for making beer pickles.

Thanks to the yeast in beer, beer pickles provide quite a nice umami flavour even when using only one vegetable such as hakusai (wombok). I like hakusai, so I often buy a whole one. But it is big, right? I use some for nabe (hotpot) dishes, some for miso soup, some for other hakusai pickles and kimchi ...

This recipe for beer pickles is one of the famous pickles from my mum's hometown. When I make this pickle, I find myself reminiscing about my mum's snowy home and the people there.

1. Cut the wombok into bite-sized pieces. Place the pieces on a zaru (flat bamboo basket) or in a large colander and allow them to dry in the sun for 1–2 hours. Finely chop the chilli.
2. Combine the pickling ingredients in a bowl, mixing well until the sugar and salt have dissolved.
3. Place the wombok in a compostable ziplock bag and add the chilli and pickling liquid. Press out as much air as possible and seal it closed.
4. Allow the pickles to rest overnight in the refrigerator, then serve.

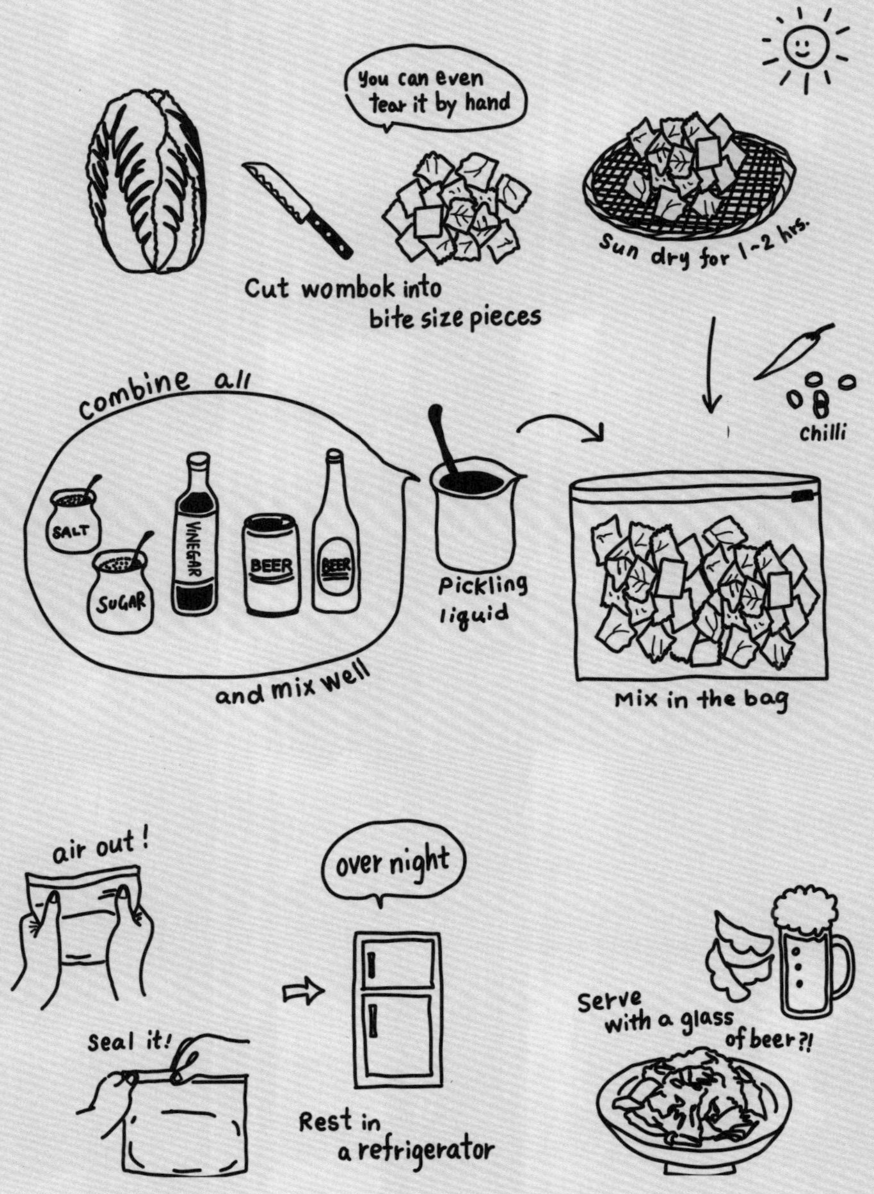
You can even tear it by hand
Cut wombok into bite size pieces
Sun dry for 1-2 hrs.
combine all
SALT
SUGAR
VINEGAR
BEER
BEER
and mix well
Pickling liquid
chilli
Mix in the bag
air out!
Seal it!
over night
Rest in a refrigerator
Serve with a glass of beer?!

KASUZUKE

粕漬け

In Japan the word 'kasu' can carry an unpleasant nuance in many contexts, but in the realm of pickling it brings to mind the deliciousness of sake kasu (also known as sake lees). Kasu (lees) is a byproduct of the sake brewing process and consists of the rice and yeast left over after sake has been fermented and pressed. Despite being the solid residue from sake production, sake kasu is rich in flavour and nutrients, making it a valued ingredient in various dishes and seasonings. Its use helps minimise waste by transforming a byproduct into a flavourful component.

Sake kasu is not only enjoyed in cooking and beverages, it also shines in pickles. Its rich flavour and slight alcohol content impart an adult taste to pickles, making them incredibly satisfying. Just one slice can tempt you to enjoy multiple bowls of rice, thanks to its deep and robust flavour.

Sake kasu can often be found in the frozen section of Japanese grocery stores. Alternatively, if you enjoy making sake at home, you can use your own sake kasu.

For a perfect combination, pair kasu pickles with sake.

KASUDOKO – THE ALL-ROUND PICKLING PASTE

粕床

You will need

300 g (10½ oz) sake kasu (sake lees)
40 g (1½ oz) miso
20 g (¾ oz) sugar
40 ml (1¼ fl oz) sake
30 ml (1 fl oz) mirin
6 g salt

STORAGE: *Store kasudoko in a clean container in the freezer for up to 6 months.*

Once you make kasudoko – the pickling paste made using sake kasu – you'll find it very handy. Kasudoko adds umami, sweetness and saltiness. It's a beautiful paste that can be used in a variety of ways. Use it to pickle vegetables, fish and meat. You can even add it to your winter soup. I like to use it as a cracker spread or dip for vegetable sticks. It's creamy and cheesy – I like the richness.

This kasudoko is the bed for pickling. Basically, just bury whatever you want to pickle in the kasudoko. After a while, the repeated pickling of vegetables will cause the paste to become softer from the vegetable moisture. Therefore, it's best to get rid of the moisture in the vegetables before you pickle them. I found an easy way to deal with this: when you want to pickle something, take a spoonful of the paste and apply it all around the vegetable you want to pickle. That way, the paste consistency stays the same. You can, of course just bury your vegetables. It's always fun to bury!

I keep the kasudoko in the freezer – there's no need to defrost it as it doesn't become hard.

1. Use a suribachi (Japanese mortar) or a bowl to combine the ingredients. You can also use a food processor, if you like. The firmness of the sake lees will differ from brand to brand. If it looks too hard, add some more sake or mirin to make it softer. If the sake lees looks soft already, maybe you will need less sake or mirin. The target texture is like a soft miso paste. You can adjust the sweetness to your preference as well.
2. It's ready to use straight away to make kasuzuke. Transfer the leftover paste to a clean container and keep it in the freezer.

CONTINUED →

YOKO'S GUIDE TO KASUZUKE

1 VEGETABLE KASUZUKE

YOKO'S RECOMMENDATIONS: asparagus spears, bell pepper (capsicum), broccolini, carrot, celery, cucumber, turnip and zucchini (courgette).

For vegetables that can be enjoyed raw, the first step is to sprinkle them with salt (1 % of the vegetable weight) and massage them to draw out some of their moisture. Allow the vegetables to rest for 5–10 minutes, until their moisture is released, then drain off any excess liquid.

If you choose to use vegetables that taste better when cooked, blanch them first in lightly salted boiling water until just cooked, then allow them to cool.

Take a spoonful or two of the kasudoko paste and apply it around the vegetables. (Alternatively, bury them in the kasudoko directly.)

Allow the vegetables to rest in the refrigerator for 1–2 days.

If you like, lightly wipe the kasudoko off the vegetables before serving, although I enjoy my vegetables with the kasudoko paste left on.

2 FISH & MEAT KASUZUKE

YOKO'S RECOMMENDATIONS: any white fish fillets, mackerel, Spanish mackerel, salmon, squid, chicken or pork.

FISH: Apply salt to both sides of the fish fillets, then allow them to rest for 15–20 minutes. Wipe the moisture off the fillets with paper towel, then cover them with a thin layer of kasudoko. Place them in a clean container and allow them to rest in the refrigerator for 1–3 days.

(Salt has the effect of drawing out moisture, causing water to come to the surface of the fish due to osmotic pressure. This moisture contains components that contribute to the fishy odour, so wiping it off can help reduce the smell. Additionally, removing excess moisture concentrates the umami flavour of the fish and prevents the kasudoko flavour from becoming diluted when making kasuzuke, resulting in a more delicious finish.)

SQUID: Wipe the moisture off the squid with paper towel, then cover it with a thin layer of kasudoko. Place it in a clean container and allow to rest in the refrigerator for 3–7 days.

CHICKEN: Breast, thigh and chicken tenders all work well. Prick the meat with a fork in five or six places and sprinkle it with a small amount of salt. This will help the flavour soak in. Cover the meat pieces with a thin layer of kasudoko, then place them in a clean container and allow to rest in the refrigerator for 1–3 days. The result will be moist and juicy.

When you're ready to cook your meat or fish, grill (broil) or pan-fry them in the usual way, but keep a close eye on them as they can burn easily.

WASABI LEAVES KASUZUKE

葉わさびの粕漬け

PICKLING TIME: *3 days*

You will need

50 g (1 ¾ oz) wasabi leaves with stems

pinch of salt

Pickling paste

50 g (1 ¾ oz) sake kasu (sake lees)

20 ml (¾ fl oz) mirin

5 g miso

2 g sugar (optional)

STORAGE: *Store in a clean container in the refrigerator for up to 1 month.*

I grow wasabi in my garden and have found that while growing wasabi roots can be challenging and requires ideal conditions, the plants themselves are relatively easy to cultivate. This pickle recipe uses the leaves and stems of the wasabi plant. The combination of the crunchy texture and distinctive heat of wasabi, along with the rich flavour of sake kasu, makes this a very popular pickle in Japan, loved for its mature, complex flavour.

Savouring wasabi leaves kasuzuke little by little is delicious. I put a small amount on the tip of my chopstick and enjoy the flavour and taste. It makes a perfect accompaniment to sake. You can also enjoy it as a dip, as is, or mix it with mayonnaise. Spread it on crackers, eat it with avocado or other sliced pickles or add some to slices of ham. And, as it is wasabi, you can enjoy it just like horseradish. Yes! Enjoy it with steaks or in sandwiches. Wasabi leaves kasuzuke give you a kick of wasabi flavour, but it also gives you a lovely creaminess.

1. Cut the wasabi leaves into 10–15 cm (4–6 in) lengths.
2. Blanch the leaves in boiling water for no more than 10 seconds, then immediately plunge them into cold water to preserve their hotness and crispness.
3. Squeeze the water from the leaves, then place them in a bowl and massage the leaves with the salt for 1–2 minutes.
4. Place the leaves in a clean container and allow them to rest at room temperature for 1 day to develop more heat. (I enjoy wasabi heat!)
5. To prepare the pickling paste, use a suribachi (Japanese mortar) or a bowl to mix the sake kasu, mirin and miso together. Taste it. If you like a bit more sweetness, add some sugar and stir to combine.
6. Remove the leaves from the container and chop them into small pieces. Squeeze the leaves again to get rid of any remaining liquid.
7. Place the wasabi leaves back into the container and add the pickling paste. Combine well and pop on a lid.
8. Allow the pickles to rest in the refrigerator for at least 3 days before serving.

SALT
cut them into 10-15cm (4-6in)
Super quick
10 sec.
Cold water
Squeeze
Leave it for a day
Chop them into small pieces
Squeeze again
Add to the paste
Prepare Kasu paste
酒粕
MIRIN
MISO
SUGAR
Mix all in Suribachi
Leave it for 3days before serving
Enjoy adult flavour ♡

NARAZUKE

奈良漬け

FERMENTATION TIME:
3 months–1 year

You will need

2 kg (4 lb 6 oz) shirouri (oriental pickling melon) or any savoury melon, such as hairy melon or choko (you can also pickle cucumber and ginger with the melon)

400 g (14 oz) salt (20 % of the vegetable weight)

Pickling paste

2 kg (4 lb 6 oz) sake kasu (sake lees)

400 g (14 oz) sugar (20 % of the sake kasu); if you have a sweet tooth you can double this amount

20–50 ml (¾–1 ¾ fl oz) mirin (optional)

STORAGE: *Store in a clean container in a dark place for up to 1 year. After 1 year transfer the contents to a small container and store in the refrigerator.*

This is one of the significant kasuzuke. It is an extremely time-consuming pickle, taking at least three months, but it can be aged for up to five years, making it a truly special delicacy. The beautiful dark brown colour comes from the length of the pickling time. The flavour is quite intense, so just one or two slices are perfect, providing a deep taste that pairs wonderfully with rice.

You can taste the sake, or alcohol, in this pickle and it was definitely a bit too much for me when I was little. However, I enjoyed a small bite and I still wanted to taste it every time we had the pickle. As I grew older I become increasingly enamoured with narazuke. Just thinking about it makes my mouth become watery.

To make 'proper' narazuke you should change the sake kasu paste a few times during pickling, but I use this easy method, which doesn't require changing the paste. It still works and it's still yummy.

Shirouri, cucumber and ginger are popular vegetables to use for narazuke.

1. Wash the melon thoroughly, then trim the ends. Cut it in half lengthways, then use a spoon to carefully scoop out the seeds and fluffy bits. Use paper towel to wipe the moisture off the melon. Place the melon pieces cut-side up on several zaru (flat bamboo baskets) or in large colanders and allow them to air-dry in a well-ventilated, shaded area for half a day to a full day.
2. Sprinkle a thin layer of salt on the bottom of a large pickling container, then rub a generous amount of salt into the hollows of the melon. Place a layer of melon in the container cut-side up and sprinkle with a little more salt.
3. After arranging the first layer, place a second layer at a 90 degree angle to the first. Continue alternating the orientation with each layer.
4. Once all the layers are arranged, sprinkle the remaining salt evenly over them. Place an inner lid on top, followed by a weight at least twice as heavy as the vegetables (in this case, 4 kg/8 lb 13 oz). If the weight sticks out from the container and the lid doesn't sit properly, cover the container with a plastic bag and newspaper, securing it tightly to keep out dust and debris.

CONTINUED →

5. Allow the pickles to rest in a cool, dark place. Within a day or two the melon will release enough liquid to cover all the vegetables. When this happens, reduce the weight by half (in this case, 2 kg/4 lb 6 oz). Put the lid on again and leave it for a week. If the liquid hasn't risen to cover all the vegetables within 2 days, increase the weight slightly and monitor the situation.
6. After 1 week, open the container and quickly rinse the salted melon under water.
7. Dry the melon thoroughly with paper towel. Arrange the pieces on zaru or in colanders and allow them to air-dry in a well-ventilated, shaded area for half a day to a full day.
8. While you're waiting for the melon to dry, combine the sake kasu with the sugar in a suribachi (Japanese mortar) or a bowl. If the sake kasu is too firm and difficult to mix, add a bit of mirin to soften it.
9. Line the inside of the pickling container with a large plastic bag. Spread 2–3 cm (¾–1¼ in) of the sake kasu mixture at the bottom of the bag before adding a layer of melon, cut-side down, ensuring they don't overlap. Evenly spread more sake kasu mixture over the melon, filling all the gaps.
10. Place another layer of melon, cut-side down, and another layer of paste. (If you've used cucumbers and ginger, place them in the gaps.)
11. Continue until you have used all of the melon, then spread the remaining paste evenly over the top. Squeeze the air out of the plastic bag and seal it, then add a lid.
12. Allow the pickles to rest in a cool, dark place. You can start eating the narazuke after about 3 months. If the pickling period is too short, the narazuke may be too salty, so leave them to ferment for longer.
13. To enjoy, simply remove the quantity you want to eat and leave the rest in the paste. To serve, you can either leave some of the paste on the narazuke or, if you prefer, lightly rinse or scrape clean, then slice.

— *NOTE*: I typically prepare this pickle with melon and cucumbers in the summer (when they are in season) and start eating them in winter. The flavour improves with time and the colour gradually deepens to a beautiful dark hue. By the time the following summer arrives, the quantity will be reduced, so I transfer the remaining pickles to a small container and store them in the refrigerator. Enjoy the changing flavour, colour and texture over time.

pickling melon
20%
SALT
scoop out the seeds
wipe!
Let them dry ...
at 90°
rub salt
the first layer
the second layer

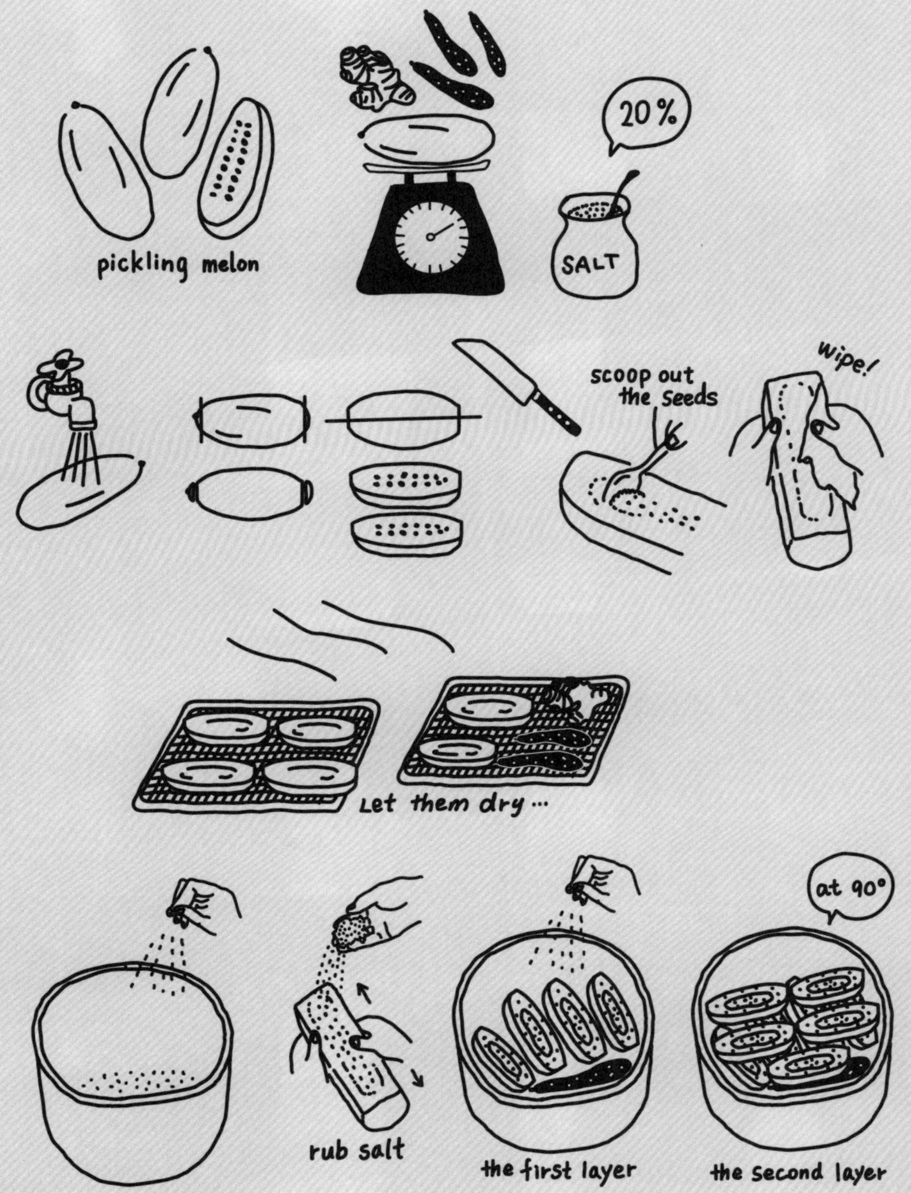

CONTINUED →

Sprinkle the remaining salt
Put the inner lid on
The liquid cover the vegetables?
1 week
Rinse!
Pat!
Dry!
Halve the weight
Sake Lees
酒粕
add Mirin if the paste is too firm
MIRIN
SUGAR
20% of Sake Lees
Line with a plastic bag

Cut side
down
Sake kasu mixture
at the bottom
Cover them with
Sake kasu mixture
Next layer
and repeat the process
air out
and tie the bag
3 months ?
6 months ?
A year ?
Put a lid on and wait
Take out
only the portion
you want to eat
Lightly rinse!
Slice & serve

KOJIZUKE

糀漬け

Koji plays a crucial role in Japanese cuisine. The word *koji* is written with characters that mean 'rice + flower', which perfectly describes the way the edible koji mold (*Aspergillus oryzae*) grows on rice. When the mold spores spread across the rice it looks as if tiny flowers are blooming. How cute! Most of Japan's fermented seasonings, such as miso, mirin and rice vinegar, are made using fermented koji. Sake is also brewed using koji. Without koji, it would be impossible to create the essential seasonings that form the foundation of Japanese food. One could even say that many of Japan's signature flavours owe their existence to koji. Thank you, koji!

In addition to seasonings, koji is used abundantly in pickles, which are called kojizuke. During the fermentation process, koji produces a wide variety of enzymes. When these enzymes break down carbohydrates they create sweetness, which gives koji pickles a mild flavour, allowing you to gently savour the natural sweetness and aroma of the koji. Kojizuke have been loved by people for generations thanks to the deliciousness imparted by koji.

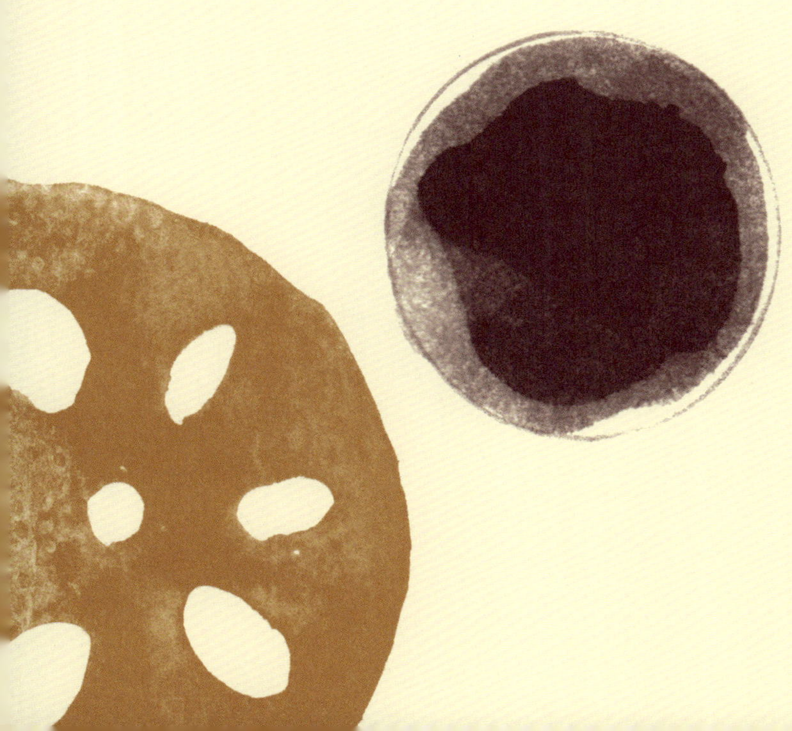

TAKUAN MADE WITH KOJI

糀で漬けるたくあん

FERMENTATION TIME:
3 weeks

This takuan pickle, made with rice koji rather than rice bran (see page 233), is our family favourite. It appears on our table every day during winter. Fresh, crunchy, juicy, not too salty, not too sweet, umami – the flavour balance is perfect. We all know this flavour is really thanks to my dad, who grows beautiful daikon, and my mum, who turns the daikon into beautiful pickles. The daikon my dad grows are enormous, about the size of my thigh. Because these daikon are huge and really heavy, it takes effort to pull them out of the ground. Transporting them after the harvest is also a challenge – my parents tie the daikon to the back of their bicycles. They can only carry five daikon at one time, otherwise it is not safe to ride. Despite the effort, this takuan pickle is truly delicious.

While we used to dry the daikon before pickling, we now follow the salting method of pre-pickling without drying. According to my mum, as she ages and her teeth become less strong, the texture of this version is easier to enjoy. If you prefer the classic texture of takuan, you might want to stick to the drying method rather than pre-pickling salting. It's fascinating how the texture changes based on whether you dry or salt the vegetables, even though both methods remove moisture.

This takuan is a hit with both relatives and friends, and my mum makes plenty of them to share with everyone, bringing much joy. I particularly enjoy the refreshing flavour of the whole yuzu that's added. We prepare it in winter – when the daikon is much juicier and sweeter – and savour it until spring.

You can easily find rice koji (frozen or dried) at Japanese grocery stores or online.

CONTINUED →

1

PRE-PICKLING

下漬け

You will need

2 kg (4 lb 6 oz) daikon with leaves
60 g (2 oz) salt (3 % of daikon weight)

1. Wash the daikon and cut off the leaves. Put the leaves aside to use later. Peel the daikon – you can use the peel in other dishes such as kinpira. Depending on the size of the daikon, cut it into a manageable size. You can cut it in half lengthways, or if it is a particularly big one (like my dad's daikon), cut it in half first and then cut it in half lengthways.
2. Rub some salt all over the daikon, then pack the daikon pieces tightly into a large pickling container. Place the reserved daikon leaves on top, then sprinkle with the remaining salt. Place an inner lid on top, followed by a weight that is twice as heavy as the daikon (in this case, 4 kg/8 lb 13 oz). Place a lid on top of this if you have one, otherwise cover the container with a plastic bag and newspaper, securing it tightly to keep out dust and debris.
3. Allow the daikon to rest in a cool, dark place. Within 1–2 days the daikon will release enough liquid to cover the vegetables. Leave it for another 2–3 days, to release more water from the daikon.

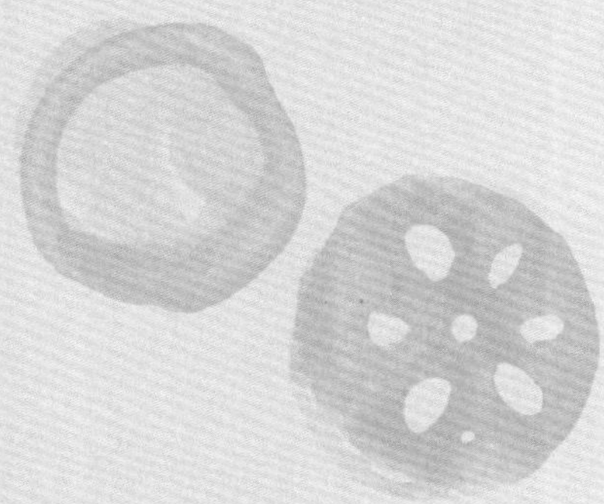

2

MAIN FERMENTATION

本漬け

You will need

Koji mixture
110 g (4 oz) rice koji
40 g (1 ½ oz) sugar
10 g salt (if you are in a warm location, increase it to 15 g/½ oz)
2 g ground turmeric (optional)

Optional flavourings
1–2 × 5 cm (2 in) squares of dried kombu
1–2 red chillies
sun-dried peel of 1–2 apples (see page 236)
sun-dried peel of 1–2 persimmons (see page 236)
1–2 whole yuzu

1. Remove the daikon from the container and discard the liquid. Clean the container thoroughly, then wipe it dry with a clean cloth.
2. For the koji mixture, combine the rice koji, sugar and salt in a small bowl. If you'd like your takuan to have a yellow finish, mix in the turmeric at this stage.
3. Prepare your optional pickle flavourings. Finely slice the kombu. The chillies are added to prevent spoilage rather than add heat, so even if you are not a fan of spicy food (like me) you can still add them. You can either add them whole or cut them in half, remove the seeds and chop them into small pieces. (Of course, if you enjoy spiciness, feel free to include the seeds as well or add some more.)
4. Sprinkle one or two handfuls of the koji mixture into the clean pickling container. Pack the daikon in a single layer on top, then sprinkle with another one or two handfuls of the koji mixture.
5. If using extra flavouring ingredients, add half of them now. If using yuzu, squeeze it over the pickling container to release the juice, then add the whole yuzu as is. (My mum is wild, so she just squeezes the yuzu by hand for this pickle, but if you would prefer a more careful approach, you can cut the yuzu in half, remove all the seeds, juice using a citrus juicer, then add both the juice and the spent yuzu.
6. Next, arrange another row of daikon, then sprinkle the remaining koji mixture on top and add any remaining optional ingredients.
7. Finally, place the pickled daikon leaves on top. Place an inner lid on top of the daikon leaves, followed by a 2 kg (4 lb 6 oz) weight.

CONTINUED →

8. Allow the pickles to rest in a cool, dark place for 2 weeks. Even after the initial liquid has been released, more moisture will continue to come out, surprisingly. Once the liquid reaches the top, reduce the weight by half.
9. To serve, remove the quantity you want to eat and lightly rinse the takuan to remove the koji mixture, if you like. Cut into slices and serve. I like to add a few of the green leaves, some apple peel and a little yuzu skin, all finely sliced.

STORAGE: *Store in a clean container in the refrigerator for up to 3 months.*

— *NOTES*: The sun-dried apple and persimmon peels improve the aroma of this pickle, but not having them doesn't mean you can't make it. There is no need to be too particular about it.

Depending on the size of the container you use, you may only need one layer of daikon, or you may need two, three or more layers. The number of layers is not important. The point is that the koji mixture is well distributed and there's some extra on top. And ... we have gravity! I tend to use more koji mixture at the higher layers because it works its way down eventually.

When you prepare this pickle in winter it will last until spring without putting it in the refrigerator. If you live in a warmer climate, it's a good idea to increase the amount of salt used when you make the koji mixture.

TAKUAN MADE WITH KOJI

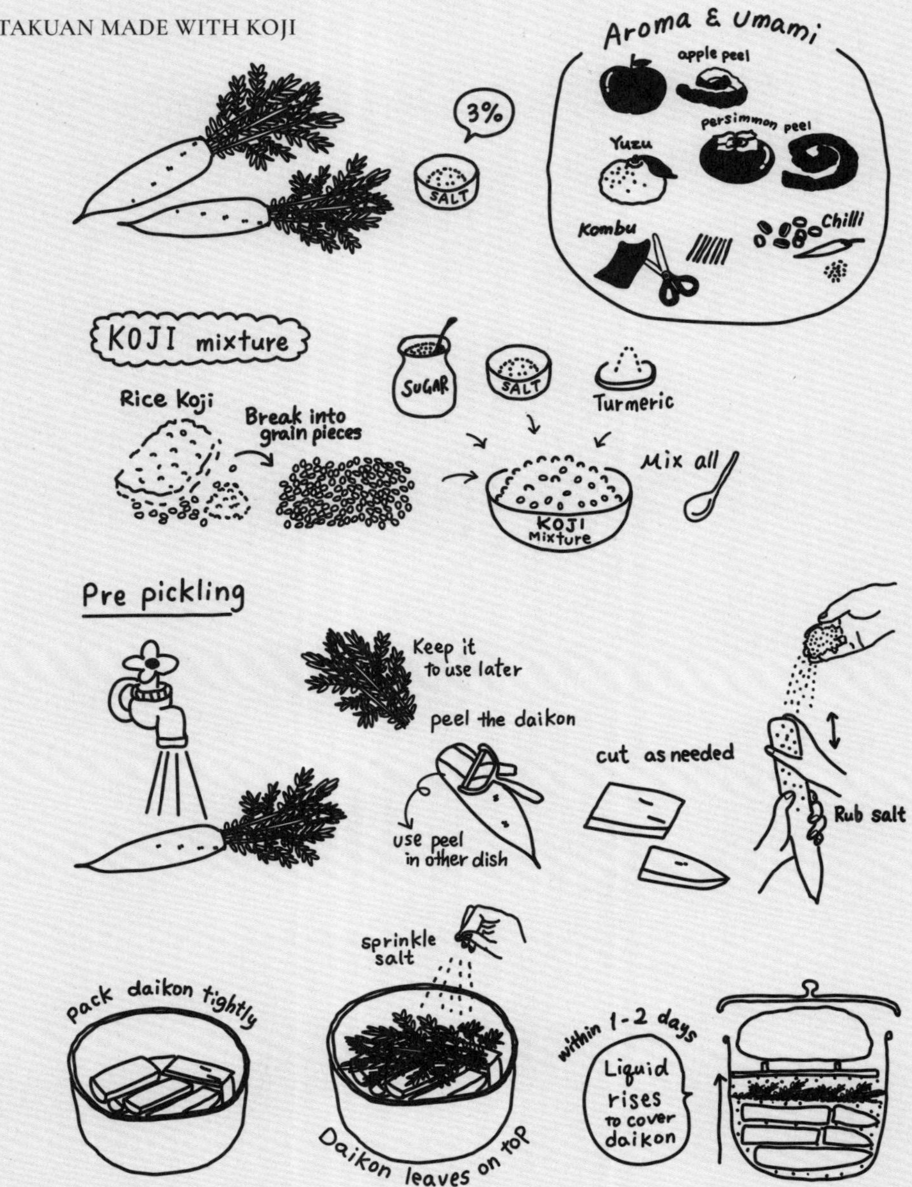

How to make kinpira with daikon skin

大根の皮で作るきんぴら

Julienne the daikon skin. Heat 1 teaspoon of sesame oil in a frying pan over medium heat and fry the peel for 3–4 minutes, until it becomes translucent. Remove the peel from the heat and season to taste with soy sauce and a dash of mirin, if you prefer a sweeter flavour. To serve, sprinkle some toasted sesame seeds and/or shichimi togarashi on top. (You can use other vegetable peels too. I sometimes use leftover pumpkin (winter squash) skin when I've made pumpkin soup.)

Take out pre-pickled daikon
Clean the container
wipe it dry
Sprinkle koji mixture at bottom
Pack daikon
Sprinkle more koji mixture on top
after squeezing, put the whole Yuzu in!!
Squeeze
add aroma & umami elements
Repeat the process until all daikon is packed
Daikon leaves on top
Ferment for 2 weeks
Take out only the portion you eat
Keep the rest in the paste
serving suggestion

SAGOHACHI 3:5:8 ZUKE

三・五・八漬け

FERMENTATION TIME:
5 hours

You will need
vegetables, such as Japanese cucumber, carrot, turnip and cherry tomatoes

Sagohachi paste
400 g (14 oz) short- or medium-grain rice or glutinous rice
200 g (7 oz) rice koji
60 g (2 oz) salt

STORAGE: *Store in a container in the refrigerator for up to 3 months.*

This pickle is a specialty from my mum's hometown in the northeast region of Japan. First, you'll need to make sagohachi paste. *Sagohachi* translates to '3, 5, 8' – these numbers represent the ratio of the three ingredients: 3 (*san*) portions of salt, 5 (*go*) portions of rice koji and 8 (*hachi*) portions of rice. Once you've prepared the sagohachi you can pickle any vegetables in the paste, quickly creating delicious and nutritious pickles. Depending on the size of your vegetables, it only takes 5–6 hours to pickle. Handy! It's not just for vegetables – you can also use it to season fish and meat, too.

Sagohachi has long been highly valued in Japan for its extended shelf life. This is thanks to the fermentation process and the salt content. However, times have changed, and modern society involves much less physical labour than in the past, leading to a demand for salt-reduced options. Nowadays, most preserved foods, including sagohachi, are made with a lot less salt. This recipe is a salt-reduced version, so the ratios are not the traditional 3:5:8.

I will show you two different ways to make sagohachi – the traditional method and a quick version. I recommend making the quick version if you live in a warm region, as sagohachi pickles originated in a cold environment where they require a fermentation time of 1 month.

1. To make the sagohachi paste, cook the rice and let it cool to body temperature. Break up the rice koji into grains, then add it to the rice and mix in well. When it has cooled completely, add the salt and mix thoroughly.
2. Transfer the sagohachi paste to a container and allow it to rest in a cool, dark place for about 1 month before using. (For a quick version, see Notes on page 141.) The mixture will develop a little sweetness when it's ready.
3. When the sagohachi is ready to use, bury your choice of vegetables in the paste, making sure they are well covered. (I normally add whole or halved vegetables, depending on their size.)
4. Allow the pickles to rest in the refrigerator for 5–6 hours, or overnight, before serving.
5. To serve, lightly wipe the sagohachi off the vegetables and cut them up as you prefer.

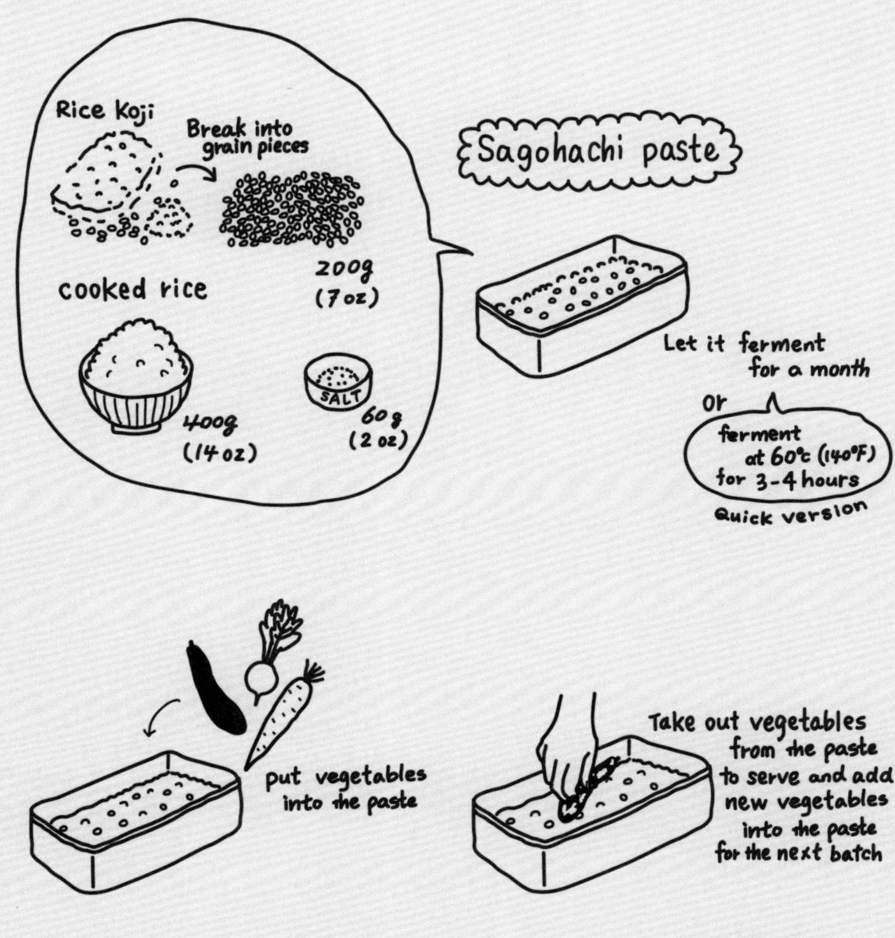

— *NOTES*: For a quick version, you'll need a rice cooker, fermenter, slow cooker, yoghurt maker, thermos or something similar that can keep the temperature stable at 60°C (140°F). Cook the rice, then let it cool to body temperature. Break up the rice koji and mix it into the rice. Now transfer the mixture to your fermenting device and keep the temperature at 60°C for 6–8 hours. When the time is up, let the rice cool completely, then add the salt and mix thoroughly. Leave it to rest for 4–6 hours, then it will be ready to use.

Sagohachi paste can be reused multiple times. I recommend adding a few vegetables to the paste every day and enjoying fresh pickles daily. After using the sagohachi many times the paste will become watery because of the moisture from the vegetables. This means the paste has less sweetness and less salt content. When the sagohachi become too watery, you can add 100 g (3½ oz) of rice koji and 25 g (¾ oz) of salt and mix it in. This way, you can keep using the sagohachi.

SANSHOZUKE

三升漬け

FERMENTATION TIME:
3 weeks

You will need (in equal amounts)
green chillies
rice koji
soy sauce or tamari

STORAGE: *Store in a clean container in the pantry for many years. My oldest jar is 3 years old. The rice koji and green chillies are amazingly yummy.*

The name of this pickle follows the same concept as 3:5:8 pickles, indicating the proportions of the ingredients. San means 3, and sho refers to the Japanese measurement. Three ingredients are used, all in equal parts. How simple! This is another famous recipe from the northern regions of Japan, including Hokkaido. The ingredients are simple: green chilli, soy sauce and rice koji. Mix equal amounts of these ingredients together and allow them to ferment. At my cooking workshops, sanshozuke is incredibly popular among people who love spicy food. The rice koji gives the spiciness a unique, mellow roundness, making it quite addictive, despite the heat. I like to add it to pasta, pop it on tofu or enjoy it with nabe (hotpot). If you're not a fan of spicy food, you can add dried daikon (see page 28). The slight sweetness from the daikon makes the flavour milder and more balanced.

1. Finely slice the green chillies into rounds. If you prefer less heat, remove all the seeds.
2. Break up the rice koji into grains and place them in a clean container. Pour in the soy sauce and add the chilli. Stir until well combined.
3. Pop on the lid and allow the mixture to rest at room temperature.
4. The next day, check the moisture content. If the rice koji has absorbed some of the soy sauce, simply add more soy sauce to just cover the chilli and mix well.
5. Over the course of about 3–4 weeks, the rice koji will gradually break down, the mixture will thicken and the rice koji will soften. At this point, it will be perfectly ready to enjoy.

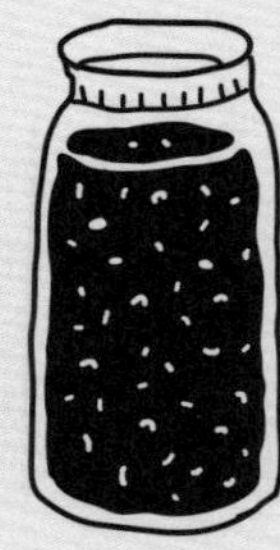

KABURA SUSHI

かぶらずし

FERMENTATION TIME:
2 weeks

Kabura sushi is a traditional fermented food used to celebrate New Year in the Hokuriku region (home to Kanazawa, a popular tourist destination). If you visit this area around New Year (or in winter), you might have the opportunity to buy kabura sushi at shops or eat it in restaurants. It is made by sandwiching salted yellowtail kingfish between salted turnips and fermenting them with rice koji. *Kabura* means turnip. It's called 'sushi' because it's a type of nare sushi (or nare zushi), which differs from the usual sushi made with vinegared rice and sashimi. Nare sushi is a traditional form of sushi where fish has been lacto-fermented with salt and rice, creating a unique flavour that preserves the fish for a long time.

I didn't taste kabura sushi until I became an adult. I'd heard about it from friends who had visited the region at just the right time and raved about how delicious and intriguing it was. For years, I wanted to try it, but never had the opportunity. Even when I saw it for sale at special regional events in Tokyo or in a department store the price was steep. It's definitely in a different league compared to, say, cucumber pickles.

One day, I thought I had to try it at least once before I died. (Okay, that's an exaggeration!) So, I booked a ticket to the Hokuriku region in winter to explore kabura sushi culture. I visited a farmer who grows a lot of turnips especially for making kabura sushi and he and his wife personally taught me the process. We actually went to the farm together, harvested the turnips in the snow, and pickled and fermented my very first kabura sushi. After that, they served me a full local meal including kabura sushi. It was so special. But they also shared a secret: local people rarely eat kabura sushi with kingfish because it is too expensive to eat daily. Instead, locals use mackerel or salmon. 'Kingfish is reserved for gifts or special guests,' they said.

There are four main steps to this recipe.

1. **Step one** (curing the fish with salt) and **step two** (pre-pickling the turnips) should be started on the same day.
2. **Step three** (preparing the amakoji) should be started 5 days later.
3. **Step four** should be started 7 days later (or 2 days after step three).

However, I've also included ways to skip a few steps (step one and step three) to make the process a bit easier by using smoked salmon and store-bought amazake. It's less pressure than to prepare everything.

CONTINUED →

1 CURING THE FISH WITH SALT

魚の塩漬け

First, cure the fish to be sandwiched between the turnips. You can use one type of fish or a few different types. If you use a variety, it will make the kabura sushi more visually appealing and the flavour will be more enjoyable. Be sure to use fresh, sashimi-grade fish.

Alternatively, you can skip this step and use smoked salmon instead.

You will need

salt

1 × 300–400 g (10½–14 oz) fillet of sashimi-grade yellowtail kingfish, salmon or mackerel

1. Generously apply enough salt to cover the fish, then wrap it tightly in plastic wrap or place it in a compostable ziplock bag and press out all of the air before sealing. Allow the fish to cure in the refrigerator for 1 week.

— *NOTE*: Traditionally, this pickle is made with fish, but since I love vegan sushi I've come up with a vegan version of kabura sushi. Instead of fish, try using pickled red and yellow bell pepper (capsicum). (Nukazuke, kasuzuke and amazu zuke bell peppers are all good.) The colours are beautiful and the flavour is very nice, too.

CONTINUED →

2 PRE-PICKLING THE TURNIPS

蕪の下漬け

The turnips need to be pre-pickled with salt before the main fermenting can begin. Salting the turnips releases moisture and makes them floppy so that the fish can be put between them. Normally really big turnips, about 13 cm (5 in) in diameter, are used for kabura sushi, but I think any size will do. This process takes about a week.

You will need
1 kg (2 lb 3 oz) turnips
30 g (1 oz) salt (3% of turnip weight)

1. Cut the tops and bottoms off the turnips – put these bits and the leaves aside for later use. If the turnips are small – around 5 cm (2 in) in diameter – slice them horizontally into 2 cm (¾ in) thick pieces. If they are larger – around 10 cm (4 in) in diameter – peel the skin thickly (you can use the skins in other dishes such as kinpira or miso soup), cut the turnips in half vertically, then slice each half into 2–3 cm (¾–1¼ in) slices.
2. Use a knife to score the centre of each turnip piece, leaving 5 mm (¼ in) from the bottom intact. I place a pair of chopsticks on either side of the turnip, so I can avoid accidentally cutting through to the bottom. The slits you make will be filled with fish later.
3. Place all the turnip pieces (including the tops, bottoms and leaves) in a clean container, then sprinkle the salt on top and mix well. Place an inner lid on top, followed by a weight 1 ½–2 times as heavy as the turnip. Place a lid on top of this. If the weight sticks out from the container and the lid doesn't sit properly, cover the container with a plastic bag and newspaper, securing it tightly to keep out dust and debris. Allow the turnip to rest in a cool, dark place for 1 week.

CONTINUED →

3 PREPARING THE AMAKOJI

甘糀作り

Amakoji is fermented sweet rice paste and it brings sweetness, umami and texture to kabura sushi. It's also called amazake (sweet sake), but it doesn't contain any alcohol or any added sugar or sweeteners. The sweetness comes from the fermentation activity. Amakoji is made with rice, rice koji and water (sometimes only with rice koji and water) and then fermented, and it has long been enjoyed as amazake, diluted with cold or hot water for a nutritious energy drink.

If you like, you can skip this step by using store-bought amazake (see Note) and move on to the main fermenting (step four). If making your own amakoji, you will need to begin the process 2 days before you start the main fermentation.

You will need
200 g (7 oz) cooked rice (short or medium grain)
200 ml (7 fl oz) water
200 g (7 oz) rice koji

1. Cook the rice normally but add a little more water to make it a little softer than usual. Once it is cooked, add the water, then allow the rice to cool to body temperature. Break up the rice koji into grains and mix them through the rice.
2. For this next step, you'll need a rice cooker, fermenter, slow cooker, yoghurt maker, thermos or something similar that can keep the temperature stable at 60°C (140°F). Transfer the rice mixture to your fermenting device and keep the temperature at 60°C (140°F) for 6–8 hours. Once it's ready, it should taste and smell sweet.
3. Allow the amakoji to mature overnight in the refrigerator before the main fermentation.

— *NOTE*: For a quick version, use 500 g (1 lb 2 oz) of store-bought 'thick' amazake or amakoji. There are three types, so make sure you read the label carefully: koji amazake (thick), which needs to be diluted before drinking; koji amazake (straight type), which can be drunk as it is; and amazake made with sake lees. Choose the first type – amazake made with koji (the thick version).

4 MAIN FERMENTATION

本漬け

Fish, turnip and amakoji. All of the main ingredients are ready. Finally we can do the main pickling. Remember, this is a winter pickle from a very cold area, so if you live in a warmer region it's probably better to ferment kabura sushi in the fridge, to let the fermentation happen slowly.

You will need
salt-cured fish (see page 147)
vinegar mixed with sake at a ratio of 5:2 to cover the salted fish
1 carrot
salt
1 red chilli
1 yuzu or lemon or other citrus
pickled turnips (see page 148)
amakoji (see opposite)

1. If you are using smoked salmon, skip this step and proceed to the next step. Remove the salted fish from the refrigerator, rinse it and slice it so the number of pieces matches the number of turnips. Ideally, the thickness should be about the same as the turnip slices. Think of it like a sandwich where the bread and the filling are about the same thickness. Soak the fish slices in the vinegar–sake mixture for at least 30 minutes, but ideally up to 2 hours. For a slightly sweeter flavour, you can use mirin instead of sake.
2. While you are waiting for the fish to pickle in the vinegar, prepare the vegetables. Finely julienne the carrot, then transfer to a bowl and sprinkle a good pinch or two of salt on top. Set aside. Finely slice the chilli into rounds (remove the seeds if you prefer less heat). Set aside. Cut a strip of peel off the yuzu, but don't include any pith as it is bitter. Finely slice the strip of peel and set aside.
3. Remove the turnips from the pre-pickling container and place them in a colander to drain any excess liquid off. Do not rinse the turnips.
4. Insert the fish or smoked salmon into the slits of the pre-pickled turnip pieces. Set aside.
5. Place a thin layer of amakoji on the bottom of a large, clean container. You will use more amakoji in the subsequent layers, so only use a small amount on the bottom.

CONTINUED →

6. Tightly pack a layer of the fish-stuffed pickled turnips in the container. Fill any gaps with pickled turnip off-cuts and leaves.
7. Sprinkle some of the carrot, yuzu peel and chilli over the turnips. Top with a layer of amakoji.
8. Repeat steps 6 and 7 to layer all the ingredients, then pour the remaining amakoji on top.
9. Seal the surface with beeswax wrap. If you have a big enough sheet of kombu, you can use it as a surface sealer instead of beeswax wrap. Place an inner lid on top and add a weight (this weight doesn't need to be too heavy – just enough to add some pressure). Close with a lid, then allow it to ferment in the refrigerator for 1 week.
10. When serving, there's no need to rinse off the amakoji around the pickles. Enjoy it all together. The flavour changes slightly each day, with the true deliciousness developing at around day 10.

STORAGE: *Store in the refrigerator for up to 10 days.*

— *NOTE*: After you eat all the kabura sushi, if you have some amakoji mixture left in the container you can use it to pickle other veggies, fish or meat. Or you can use it as a seasoning. This paste is thoroughly fermented and rich in turnip extract, making it packed with both lactic acid bacteria and umami. Make sure to use every bit of it, leaving nothing to waste.

Salting the fish
Sashimi
3%
SALT
1 week
Pre-pickling the turnip
Pickle these parts too
3%
SALT
small
Large
within 2-3 days
Liquid rises to cover turnip
pickling container is also handy
Preparing the Ama Koji
Rice Koji
Break into grain pieces
cooked rice
water
Mix all & ferment for 6-8 hours
60°C
Keep it in a fridge overnight
Finishing up the fish
Pickle the fish
5 : 2
VINEGAR
+
SAKE
OR
MIRIN
Start pickling
Open the pickled turnip and insert the pickled fish

Fish-stuffed pickled turnips
Carrot
Yuzu skin
Chilli
all ingredients
are ready
Ama koji
off cuts
leaves
Place Ama koji
at the bottom
pack the turnips
Fill the gaps with leaves
and off cuts
Sprinkle carrots,
yuzu and chilli
Pour Ama koji on top
Repeat layering
if needed
Seal with Kombu or
beeswax wrap
Cut into
reasonable sizes
to serve

MISOZUKE

味噌漬け

Misozuke refers to anything pickled in miso. How simple is that? It's not only for vegetables – anything can be pickled in miso – tofu, eggs, fish and meat. You might have heard of saikyozuke (fish pickled in saikyo miso, the sweet white miso), which is a famous dish from Kyoto. Saikyozuke is one type of misozuke. Because misozuke are so simple, the miso's quality and flavour matters. Traditionally, only miso was used, but nowadays mirin or sugar is often added to make them milder. Some people also add sake kasu (sake lees) to add more flavour.

Historically, miso pickles were made to prevent food going bad. The preservative power of miso was so effective that they were especially valuable during seasons when vegetables were not available. My mother, who is from the snowy Tohoku area, often talks about how in cold regions people would preserve certain foods to sustain their diet through the winter until the snow melted in spring.

Misozuke are still widely made in many households because they are so yummy. But miso is also still used as a preservative. I use it for preserving raw garlic when I harvest it. Not only does this infuse the garlic with the flavour of the miso (in fact, it makes both the miso and the garlic more delicious), but it also preserves the garlic without sprouting.

In this chapter, we'll explore two types of miso pickling: a versatile miso doko for enjoying quick misozuke; and a long-term misozuke designed for extended preservation.

Miso pickles made with a basic miso doko are typically ready in less than a week, with most ready to enjoy in just a few hours. Once the miso doko is prepared, you can use it to pickle vegetables, tofu or any ingredient of your choice – there are no limits to what you can pickle! Since the pickling period is short, these are easy, hassle-free pickles you can make whenever the idea strikes. However, as you keep using the miso doko repeatedly, it will gradually become watery, so you'll need to adjust its consistency as needed.

In contrast, long-term miso pickles require months of pickling. Once you start, you can leave them to develop their flavour for several months – just don't forget about them! The result is a deeply flavourful pickle, nurtured by time. They are absolutely mouthwatering.

While misozuke are perfect with rice, they also pair wonderfully with other dishes. Try them finely chopped and combined with cheese on crackers or mixed through a salad. They can be a delightful snack and go perfectly with a glass of wine.

PREPARING MISO DOKO FOR QUICK MISOZUKE

基本の味噌床

You will need
200 g (7 oz) miso
100–200 ml (3½–7 fl oz) mirin (the volume will depend on your miso's firmness) or sake if you use a sweet type of miso
10 g sugar (if your miso is salty)
pinch of salt

The medium for making quick misozuke is called miso doko. Misozuke prepared using miso doko are convenient because they can be prepared quickly and enjoyed like a salad. Even with a short pickling time they are a living food full of enzymes and lactic acid bacteria.

The flavour of the miso doko depends on the sort of miso you use, and this will impact the flavour of your miso-pickled vegetables. I think this is great – we can enjoy all the differences. You can adjust the sweetness of miso doko to suit your palate. How? Take a little bit of paste and taste it. Do you like it? Then that's good! Some might think it's too salty – if so, add some sugar. The texture of the miso doko should be like yoghurt, so you may need to adjust it by adding some more mirin or sake until it is nice and spreadable.

Preparing miso doko is pretty easy and you can use the miso doko repeatedly. The miso doko will eventually become watery because of the moisture from the vegetables. When this happens, try pickling dried vegetables such as dried daikon (see page 28), dried shiitake mushrooms and dried tofu (see page 28). When you pickle dried foods, they absorb some of the moisture from the miso doko, helping to concentrate the texture. After repeated use of your miso doko, you might also notice the flavour has weakened. In this case, add more miso to adjust and refresh the taste. And when finally the miso doko becomes too loose, repurpose it for dressings or cooking. It also works wonderfully as a flavourful sauce.

1. Put all the ingredients in a bowl and whisk them thoroughly to make a smooth paste. Adjust the mirin or sake as needed to achieve a sauce-like consistency.
2. Transfer the miso doko to a clean container or jar and store in the refrigerator for up to 6 months.

SEASONAL VEGETABLE MISOZUKE

季節野菜の味噌漬け

PICKLING TIME: *3 hours*

You will need

any seasonal vegetables, such as carrot, bell peppers (capsicums), asparagus spears, daikon and burdock

1 × quantity Miso doko (see page 158)

STORAGE: *Store the vegetables in the miso doko in the refrigerator for up to 1 week. I recommend taking out only as much as you need.*

Simply by immersing vegetables in miso doko you can make delicious misozuke. It's a good idea to lightly salt and drain the vegetables first, especially high-water content vegetables such as cucumbers. This helps maintain the concentration of the miso. For vegetables that taste better cooked, blanch them lightly before placing them in the miso doko.

My recommended vegetables for misozuke are root vegetables such as carrots, turnips, burdock and daikon. Personally, carrots and burdock are my favourites, but any vegetable works. The ingredients listed in this recipe are just a few examples; try using any seasonal vegetables you have in your garden or find at the market.

There is a kind of balance between miso doko's saltiness (or sweetness) and the vegetables' size – you will learn by experience what is your preference. Sometimes, instead of burying vegetables directly into the miso doko, I like to add some miso doko to a glass jar and pickle vegetables I've cut into batons. Or, I put seasonal vegetables in a compostable ziplock bag and add some miso doko to the bag to coat the vegetables. These methods are easy and yummy, and avoids the miso doko becoming watery.

1. Cut the vegetables so they fit easily into your miso doko container.
2. If the vegetables can be eaten raw, such as carrot and bell pepper, add a pinch of salt and combine gently. Allow the vegetables to rest for 5 minutes to release their moisture.
3. Wipe the vegetables dry with paper towel. It's important to thoroughly remove any moisture from the vegetables at this stage to prevent the miso doko becoming watery.
4. If the vegetables are usually eaten cooked, such as asparagus, then bring a small saucepan of water to the boil, add the vegetables and lightly blanch for 1–2 minutes, then drain and place on a zaru (flat bamboo basket) or in a colander to cool.
5. Bury the vegetables in the miso doko, making sure they are completely covered. Put a lid on and allow them to rest in the refrigerator for at least 3 hours. This will give you lightly pickled vegetables (asazuke), while leaving them for 1 day will result in a richer, more deeply flavoured misozuke.
6. When you're ready to serve, gently wipe the miso doko off the surface of the vegetables and slice them into your desired shape.

Any vegetable works!!

Pickle vegetables
in the basic Miso doko

vegetables yummy as raw

cut in
good sizes

wipe!

remove
moisture

At least for
a few hours

vegetables yummy as cooked

cut in
good sizes

Blanch briefly

Bury
the vegetables
into the Miso doko

vegetable
sticks

basic Miso doko

Easy Misozuke
in a jar

有機しょうゆ
本醸造醤油の豊かな香り、味の
正田の「有機」、格別の仕上がりです

YOUNG GARLIC MISOZUKE

新にんにくの味噌漬け

PICKLING TIME: *1 day*

You will need
1–2 young garlic bulbs
100 g (3½ oz) Miso doko (see page 158), or enough to cover the garlic

STORAGE: *Store in the refrigerator for up to 1 month.*

Garlic is available year-round, but the garlic that comes out in early summer can be referred to as 'young garlic'. This garlic is juicy and has a mild pungency, which can only be enjoyed during this time of year. After harvesting garlic, I make garlic rice, fried garlic and this miszuke. Once pickled, the garlic becomes fluffy and offers a uniquely delicious flavour. By the way, regular garlic is simply the dried version of this young garlic. As it dries, its pungency increases and when pickled it becomes delicious as a condiment.

1. Separate the garlic into individual cloves. Cut the root end off each garlic clove and remove the skin.
2. Bring a saucepan of water to the boil. Add the garlic and blanch for 1–2 minutes, then drain and transfer to a zaru (flat bamboo basket) or colander to cool.
3. Once the garlic cloves have cooled completely, bury them in the miso doko, making sure they are covered.
4. Allow the garlic to rest in the refrigerator for at least 1 day before enjoying.

TOFU MISOZUKE

お豆腐の味噌漬け

FERMENTATION TIME:
1–7 days

You will need
450 g (1 lb) best-quality Japanese momen tofu
50 g (1 ¾ oz) Miso doko (see page 158)

STORAGE: *Store in the refrigerator for up to 10 days.*

The first time I ever tried miso-pickled tofu was at a koryoriya (small plate restaurant). I was living in a neighbourhood in Tokyo called Koenji at the time, and it was served as a snack alongside drinks. The owner said, 'This tofu has been pickled in miso for a week. It tastes just like cheese, doesn't it?' I remember thinking, *Tofu that tastes like cheese?* But when I took a bite, I was completely amazed by the rich, flavourful taste – it was hard to believe it was the same plain tofu I was used to. Even the slightly brownish colour on the outside was beautiful. After that first encounter with miso-pickled tofu, I began making it myself from time to time. I love both its taste and texture. I often serve it for lunch during the workshops I run, and it's always a popular dish with the participants.

The key to this dish is starting with good-quality tofu. I often make it using tofu that I've made myself from organic soybeans, but when I'm busy I use store-bought tofu. Just be sure to choose the best tofu you can find. You can use silken tofu, but it tends to fall apart more easily, so Japanese-style momen (firm or slightly firm) tofu is easier to handle. As for the miso, feel free to use your favourite kind – just make sure it's delicious!

1. First, drain the tofu. After removing it from the packet, gently wrap the tofu in muslin (cheesecloth) or paper towel, then place it on a zaru (flat bamboo basket) or similar for about 30 minutes. To speed up the draining process, you can place a plate or a small cutting board on top of the tofu and apply light pressure. Be careful not to use anything too heavy, as it may crush the tofu.
2. After draining, remove the muslin or paper towel from the tofu and gently pat it dry. Wrap the tofu again in clean muslin or paper towel and spread the miso doko over the entire surface.
3. Place the tofu in a clean container and allow it to rest in the refrigerator for at least 1 day, but you can leave it for up to a week. The length of pickling time is up to you. You can start eating it the next day, but you'll notice it becomes richer in flavour around the third day. Personally, I prefer tofu that has been pickled for 5–7 days.

— *NOTES*: Instead of applying the miso doko paste around the wrapped tofu, you can bury the wrapped tofu directly in the miso doko. Feel free to choose whichever method you prefer.

You can also use the tofu as is, without wrapping it at all. Personally, I prefer misozuke tofu without any miso sticking to the surface when serving it (most people assume it's just plain tofu, so I enjoy surprising them when they exclaim, 'What is this? This tofu is delicious!'). That said, you can also serve it with some miso from the miso doko still clinging to the surface. It's entirely up to you.

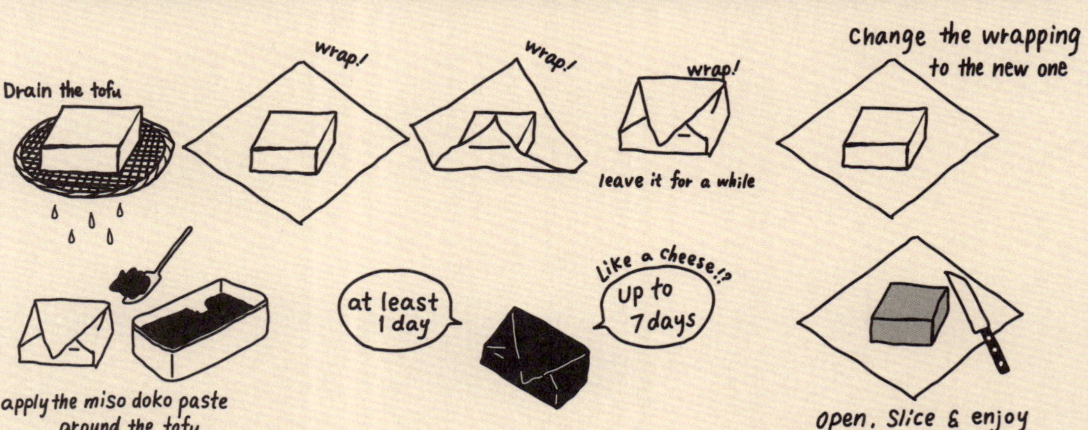
Drain the tofu
wrap!
wrap!
wrap!
leave it for a while
Change the wrapping
to the new one
apply the miso doko paste
around the tofu
at least
1 day
Like a cheese!?
up to
7 days
open, Slice & enjoy

EGG YOLK MISOZUKE

卵黄の味噌漬け

PICKLING TIME: *1–3 days*

You will need

6 eggs

100 g (3½ oz) Miso doko (see page 158)

STORAGE: *Store in the refrigerator for up to 3 days.*

There's something special about miso-pickled egg yolks. In Japan, even a raw egg in the middle of a dish makes it look delicious and actually taste better. We pickle just the yolk in miso, which has a unique appeal: the beautiful amber colour, the texture and the incredibly rich umami flavour. It's a favourite delicacy for those who enjoy drinking, but even non-drinkers like me can enjoy it with rice – it's truly satisfying. This is the magic of miso.

You can use raw yolks directly, but here's a little trick: freeze the whole egg in the shell first, then thaw them and crack them open. This gives you perfectly round yolks that look quite impressive. It's a bit of extra effort, but if presentation matters, it's worth trying it.

Of course, you can use the leftover egg whites as well. How about chiffon cake or meringues?

I use fresh farm eggs only.

1. Put the whole eggs (with shell) into a freezer bag and freeze them for 1 day. The eggshells will crack but that's okay.
2. Put three-quarters of the miso doko in a small, clean container big enough to fit the six yolks.
3. Peel the eggshells, then let the eggs sit in a bowl for a while. The yolks will eventually separate cleanly from the egg whites.
4. Place the yolks onto the miso doko. Pour the remaining miso doko over the egg yolks. Pop a lid on the container and store it in the refrigerator for at least 1 day before serving.

— *NOTES*: If you leave the egg yolks to pickle for too long, they will become too salty. It's best to eat them within 2–3 days.

This misozuke is delicious with the addition of some sake kasu (sake lees). Add 1 tablespoon of sake kasu to the miso doko and combine well.

NAGAIMO MISOZUKE

長芋の味噌漬け

PICKLING TIME: *1 day*

You will need

300 g (10½ oz) nagaimo (Japanese mountain yam)
1 small garlic clove
100 g (3½ oz) Miso doko (see page 158)

STORAGE: *Store in the refrigerator for up to 1 week.*

I love the crisp texture of nagaimo and always buy it when I see it at the market. These long, slim yams have pale whiteish-yellow skin. I enjoy it lightly stir-fried or as is, but my favourite way to eat it is as misozuke.

If you like a lighter flavour, you can start eating the nagaimo misozuke after 1 day. Personally, I think it tastes much better after 3 days or even a week.

1. Wash the nagaimo under running water, using a brush to thoroughly clean it. Pat it dry with paper towel. If you prefer, peel the skin off. You can also burn off the fine roots using the burner on a gas stove. Cut the nagaimo in half.
2. Grate the garlic clove into a bowl, then add the miso doko and whisk to combine well.
3. Place the nagaimo and the miso doko mixture in a compostable ziplock bag, press out as much as air as possible and seal it closed. Allow it to rest in the refrigerator for at least 1 day.
4. For clean presentation lightly wipe the miso doko off the surface of the nagaimo and cut it into bite-sized pieces. Alternatively, serve with a bit of miso doko as a sauce.

QUAIL EGG MISOZUKE

うずらの卵の味噌漬け

PICKLING TIME: *1 day*

You will need
10 quail eggs
1–2 garlic cloves
50 g (1 ¾ oz) Miso doko (see page 158)
pinch of shichimi togarashi or chilli flakes

STORAGE: *Store in the refrigerator for up to 5 days.*

The small, cute quail egg! When you pickle them in miso they turn into a flavoursome dish. Sometimes I receive quail eggs from neighbours and sometimes I buy them from farmers' markets. You can also make this with regular chicken eggs, they'll just be bigger.

The rich flavour of the miso combined with the richness of the eggs makes for a simple yet delicious snack. They pair beautifully with beer and sake and can even be enjoyed with a glass of wine as a substitute for cheese. The bold flavour makes them a great addition to your bento or picnic lunch box. I like to serve them as a side dish or I skewer them and serve as finger food.

1. Place the quail eggs in a saucepan, then pour in enough water to just cover them. Bring to the boil, gently, stirring the eggs by rolling them to prevent the yolk from settling unevenly. When the water begins to boil, stop stirring and let them cook for 2–3 minutes (2 minutes for soft-boiled; 3 minutes for hard-boiled).
2. Drain the eggs and place them in a bowl of cold water to cool. Meanwhile, grate the garlic.
3. When the eggs are cool, place them in a container, cover with a lid and gently shake the eggs in all directions to create fine cracks all over the shells. Peel the shells, starting from the wider end of the eggs (they're easier to peel this way).
4. Place the miso doko, eggs, garlic and shichimi togarashi in a clean container, making sure the eggs are coated in the miso doko mixture. Cover the container and allow the eggs to rest in the refrigerator for at least 1 day before enjoying.

AUNTY HARUKO'S MISOZUKE

はるこおばちゃんの味噌漬け

FERMENTATION TIME:
3–6 months

You will need

300 g (10½ oz) vegetables, such as carrot and burdock (my favourites!) or cucumber, green beans, daikon, turnip, celery or eggplant (aubergine)
9 g salt (3% of vegetable weight)
600 g (1 lb 5 oz) red miso
5–10 g bonito flakes (optional)

STORAGE: *You can store the pickles in the miso in the refrigerator for up to 1 year but they get saltier with time. Alternatively, take the pickles out of the miso paste after 3–6 months, then store them in the refrigerator in a clean container for up to 1 month.*

This miso pickle recipe is something I learned from my beloved Aunty Haruko. It's a pickle that takes time to make. Traditionally, rather than simply pickling vegetables in miso, vegetables would be placed at the bottom of the container when preparing miso before fermenting it. As the miso matured, the vegetables also gradually transformed into amber-hued pickles. These vegetables absorbed the rich flavours of both the miso and miso-tamari (the delicious liquid that forms during miso fermentation), developing a deep, savoury taste over time. Depending on how long the miso was left to mature, the pickles would be at their best after about a year.

According to Aunty Haruko, back in the day, miso and these pickles would often be sent to family members. When it arrived, the container would be layered: a bed of miso at the bottom, followed by two whole pieces of katsuobushi (those thick, branch-like blocks of dried bonito before shaving), then a bag filled with vegetables that had already been transformed into delicious pickles. On top of that, there'd be another two katsuobushi blocks, and finally, another thick layer of miso. The main thing being sent was the miso itself.

The difference in flavour between homemade and store-bought miso is undeniable. Every year, many parents sent homemade miso to their children who had moved to the city. As they used the miso, they'd eventually discover the surprise of those tasty, beautiful pickles at the bottom. This meant the vegetables were preserved for nearly 2 years before being eaten – and they only got more delicious with time. It's truly impressive how people in the past mastered both preservation and gourmet techniques.

The deeply infused flavour of vegetables that have spent so long soaking up miso is incredibly delicious. Even during the hot summer months when you don't feel like eating, a small amount of these pickles, chopped and placed on rice, will make you want to eat bowl after bowl. Aunty Haruko would often tell me about chopping the pickles into small pieces, putting them on cold rice and pouring iced water or chilled tea over them, eating them like ochazuke (a simple rice dish with tea). She would get excited every time she shared this story, and you could tell just how much she loved it.

CONTINUED →

NOTE: To sew your own cloth bag, cut two pieces of fabric the same size as your container. Place the fabric pieces on top of each other and sew together the two long sides and one short side using a simple running stitch or similar. Once you've added the vegetables, fold over the open end or sew up the bag to secure.

Of course, not many people make miso from scratch these days, so I've adapted this recipe to be easier to prepare at home using store-bought miso. The key is to buy really good-quality miso, ideally homemade miso from a local farmers' market.

The vegetables used for these pickles are typically summer vegetables, but really, you can use anything. Green beans, myoga (Japanese ginger flower buds), lotus root, daikon, burdock, carrots, shiso seeds, eggplant (aubergine), cucumber and so on.

This miso pickle tends to be rich in flavour, so it's better used as a seasoning rather than eaten on its own. It's delicious mixed with cream cheese, stirred into scrambled eggs or blended with tofu. And, of course, it's great on rice. Think of it more as a condiment or a flavour enhancer for vegetables rather than an eating pickle.

1. Chop the vegetables into small, bite-sized pieces.
2. Place the vegetables in a large bowl, sprinkle the salt on top and then mix it through thoroughly.
3. Place an inner lid on the vegetables and then a weight at least twice as heavy as the vegetables. Add an outer lid and allow them to rest for 1–2 days to draw out the moisture.
4. Once the moisture has been drawn out, wipe the vegetables dry with paper towel or a kitchen towel. (It's important to thoroughly remove any moisture from the vegetables at this stage to prevent the miso from becoming watery.)
5. Place a quarter of the miso at the bottom of a clean container. If using bonito flakes, sprinkle half on top of the miso. Place the vegetables in a thin cotton bag (see Note), then add this bag to the miso.
6. Sprinkle the remainder of the bonito flakes (if using) on the cotton bag now. Add the remaining miso as a thick layer on top.
7. Seal the surface of the miso with plastic wrap or beeswax wrap, then add the container's lid.
8. Allow the vegetables to ferment in the refrigerator for 3–6 months before using.

Any vegetables like...
even ginger and myoga are good
Chop chop
3%
SALT
For 1 to 2 days
Weight
Squeeze
Optional
Katsuobushi
Bonito stick or flakes
wipe!
put all vegetables in!
remove moisture
make an easy cotton bag
Place the stuffed bag on the Miso bed
some Miso at the bottom

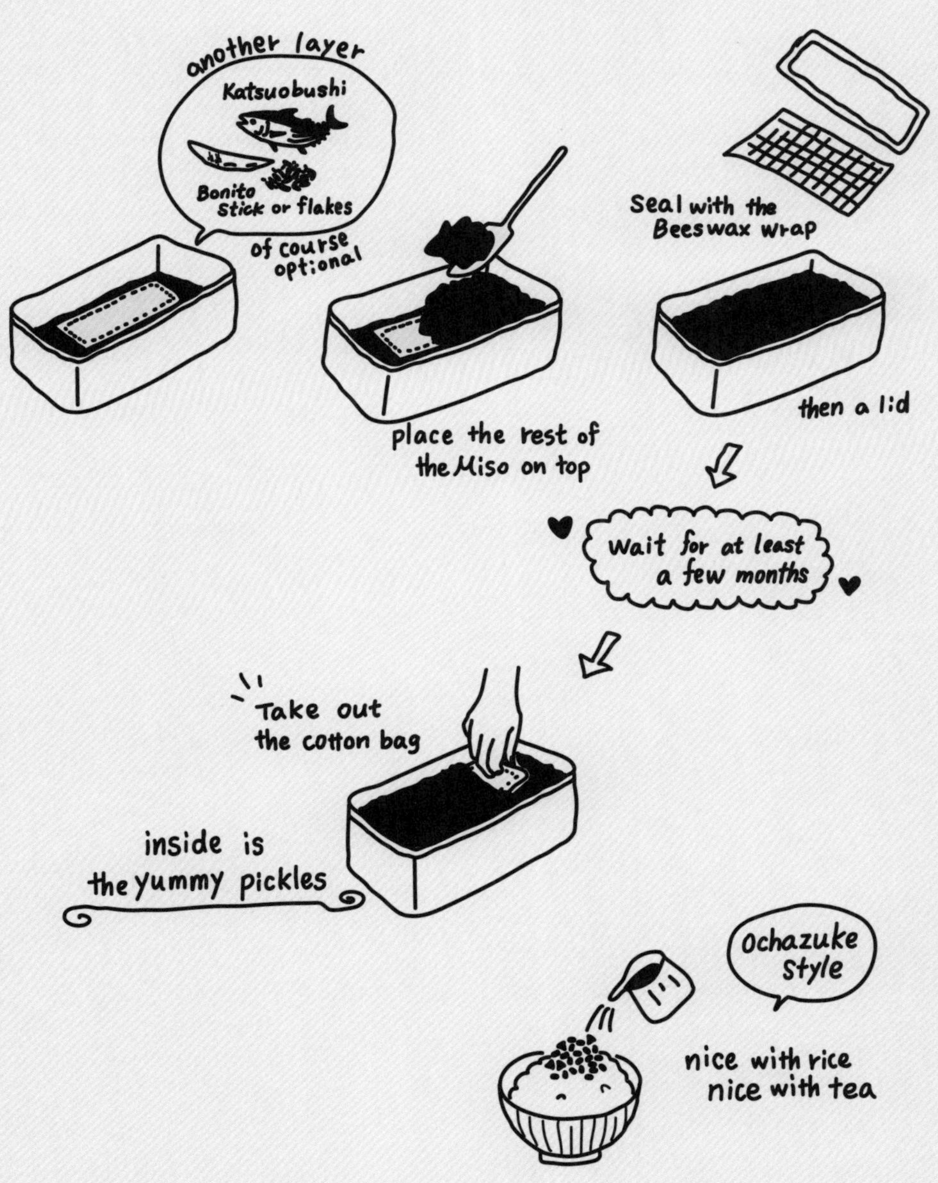
another layer
Katsuobushi
Bonito
Stick or flakes
of course
optional
place the rest of
the Miso on top
Seal with the
Beeswax wrap
then a lid
Wait for at least
a few months
Take out
the cotton bag
inside is
the yummy pickles
Ochazuke
Style
nice with rice
nice with tea

AGED GINGER MISOZUKE

生姜の味噌漬け

FERMENTATION TIME:
6 months

You will need
500 g (1 lb 2 oz) ginger (young or old)
75 g (2¾ oz) salt (15% of ginger weight)
350 g (12½ oz) miso
80–100 g (2¾–3½ oz) sugar

STORAGE: *Store in the refrigerator for up to 6 months.*

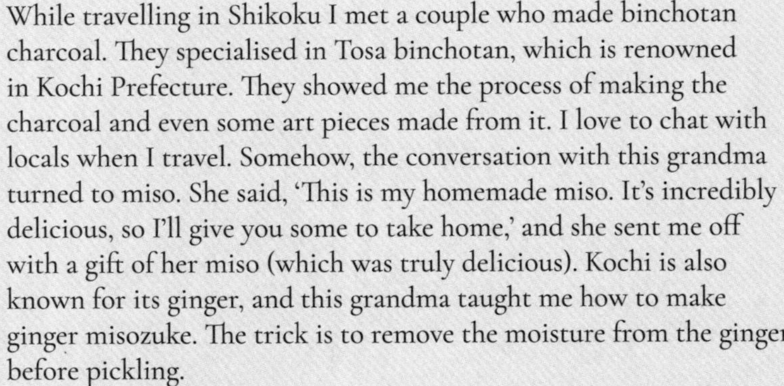
While travelling in Shikoku I met a couple who made binchotan charcoal. They specialised in Tosa binchotan, which is renowned in Kochi Prefecture. They showed me the process of making the charcoal and even some art pieces made from it. I love to chat with locals when I travel. Somehow, the conversation with this grandma turned to miso. She said, 'This is my homemade miso. It's incredibly delicious, so I'll give you some to take home,' and she sent me off with a gift of her miso (which was truly delicious). Kochi is also known for its ginger, and this grandma taught me how to make ginger misozuke. The trick is to remove the moisture from the ginger before pickling.

This pickle goes with many foods. It's the perfect match with rice, of course, but you can use it in any meal where you would normally use ginger. For example, finely chop this pickled ginger and add it to a dumpling mixture for delicious dumplings. It also teams well with pork and fish.

1. Soak the ginger in water for 1 day, then drain and use a brush to gently clean it.
2. Place the ginger and salt in a container, followed by an inner lid, then a 1 kg (2 lb 3 oz) weight. Set aside at room temperature for 3 days.
3. Rinse the ginger well, then dry it thoroughly with paper towel.
4. Lay the ginger on a zaru (flat bamboo basket) or in a colander and allow it to dry in the sun for 1 day.
5. Combine the miso and sugar in a bowl.
6. Place half the miso mixture in the bottom of a clean container. Place the ginger on top, then seal it in with the remaining miso mixture.
7. Seal the surface with plastic wrap or beeswax wrap and add a lid.
8. Allow it to rest in the refrigerator for 6 months before serving.
9. To serve, slice the ginger. You can lightly wipe off the miso, if you like, or you can leave it on.

MISO
SUGAR
Combine well
Seal the Surface with beeswax wrap
after 6 months
dig it out!
slice and serve♥

AGED GARLIC MISOZUKE

にんにくの味噌漬け
長期保存バージョン

FERMENTATION TIME:
3 months–1 year

You will need
70 g (2½ oz) garlic
200 g (7 oz) red miso (or enough to cover your garlic)

STORAGE: *Store in the refrigerator. It will be keep for many years.*

Since moving to Australia I've started growing a lot of garlic. It seems that the area where I live is well suited for garlic cultivation and, thankfully, it grows beautifully without much effort. Growing garlic only requires a single clove in the soil to produce a large bulb, and since it needs minimal care during the growing period, I find it perfect for someone as lazy as me. I plant the garlic cloves in late summer or the beginning of autumn, allowing them to develop some leaves before the frost sets in. Then, it seems to go dormant during the winter. When spring arrives, it wakes up and starts to grow. By the time summer comes, I have lovely, robust garlic.

I dry and store my garlic, but it's quite difficult to keep it from sprouting for an entire year. That's why I turn some of the harvested garlic into miso pickles. Both the garlic and miso become delicious, making it a win–win situation. The miso-pickled garlic can be chopped and eaten as is or used in cooking, while the miso becomes quite potent from the garlic. Instead of using both garlic and miso in my cooking, I opt for this garlic-flavoured miso.

Don't worry too much about the quantities listed here – they're just a rough guide. Use a jar that fits the amount of garlic you'd like to preserve, and as long as the garlic is completely covered with miso, it'll be fine. Both the miso and garlic are preserved foods, after all.

This method is intended for long-term preservation to prevent garlic from sprouting, so be sure to use aged or red miso that is suitable for extended storage.

1. Separate the garlic into individual cloves. Cut off the root end and remove the skin.
2. Transfer the miso to a clean jar. Bury the garlic cloves in the miso, making sure they are completely covered, then pop on the lid.
3. Allow the garlic to rest in a cool, dark place for at least 3 months before using.

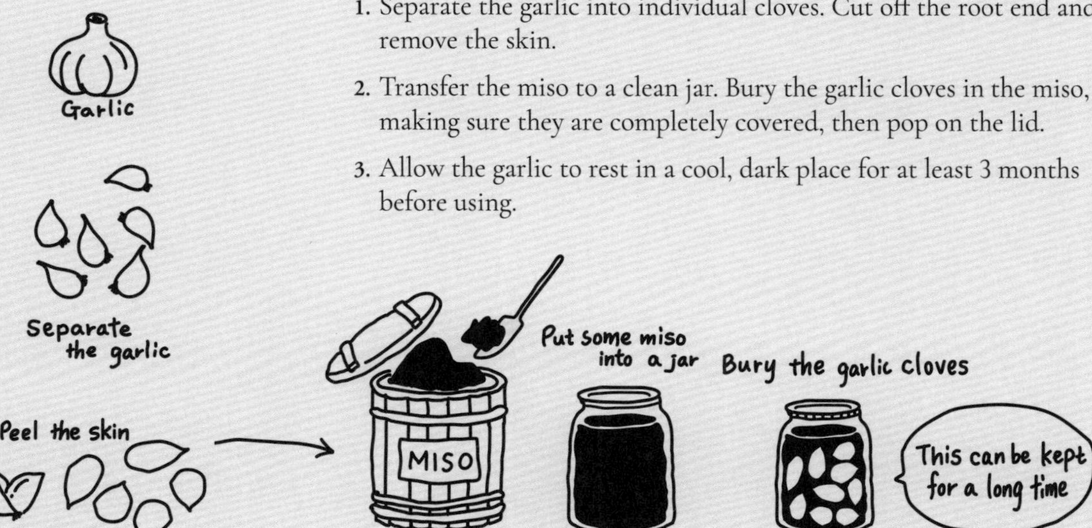

NUKAZUKE

ぬか漬け

Nukazuke are probably the most famous and popular Japanese pickles. Nuka is the nutrient-rich, light brown rice bran byproduct produced when white rice is processed. (White rice + nuka = brown rice. Nuka = brown rice – white rice. Do you get it now?) Nukazuke are pickles made using the nuka.

In order to pickle various type of vegetables, eggs, fish and meat, we prepare what we call nuka doko, which is fermented nuka paste. Nuka doko is time-consuming to make, but once it's ready you can use it as long as you like – it can last the rest of your life. One-hundred-year-old nuka doko is not that unusual. It's something that your family can keep passing to the next generation and the next generation and the next generation. I love that idea. Nuka doko lives longer than you!

Once your nuka doko is fermented and ready to use, you can pickle seasonal vegetables in a very short time – 4–6 hours, depending on the size and texture of the vegetables. As you keep pickling using the same nuka doko again and again, it will get even better. Nuka doko is something you grow and nurture, so everyone's nuka doko is different. They all have personality and they're all yummy.

Another great thing about nukazuke is the nutritional benefit. Nuka doko contains an amazing amount of living things: there are 2 billion living organisms in a piece of nuka paste the size of your pinky fingernail (I'm sure you will start talking to your nuka doko). By pickling vegetables in nuka doko they absorb the nutritious elements. So, for example, a nukazuke cucumber has a lot more nutritional value than a fresh cucumber.

Every time I go back to Japan, I enjoy my mum's nukazuke. She only uses freshly harvested vegetables from Dad's garden. My favourites are cucumber and turnip. They are really, really, really yummy. One summer when I went back home with my husband we ate so many nukazuke cucumbers – every meal, every day and as a snack with green tea – Mum was thrilled that the summer vegetables all got consumed while we stayed.

I hope you will start your nukazuke journey and enjoy the process.

There are three steps to making nukazuke, first you must prepare the nuka doko.

NUKA DOKO

ぬか床

FERMENTATION TIME:
2 weeks–1 month

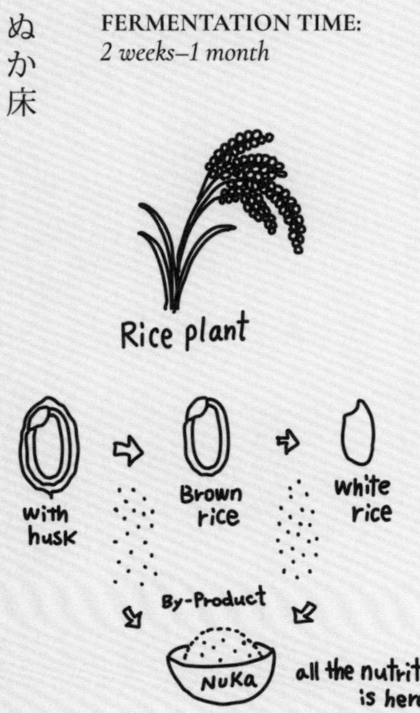

Nuka doko is comprised of rice bran, salt and water. How simple is that? Starting a new nuka doko is always exciting – almost like a New Year's resolution. If you can get some fermented nuka doko from somebody you know, you can add it to your own nuka doko to accelerate its growth. To this base nuka doko we add kombu and chilli. Kombu adds umami and the chilli assists with preservation as well as prevention of fat oxidation (rice bran contains about 20 per cent fat!). Be sure to always include both in your nuka doko.

Then, there are additional ingredients you can add to the basic nuka doko. These ingredients add additional flavours, umami, aroma and/or preservative qualities. Each of them has some sort of role. All contribute to the flavour. You don't have to add everything or anything. Basic nuka doko is good enough. I add most of the listed additional ingredients when I have them in my pantry, as I like a bit of everything and, more than anything, it's fun.

– *NOTE:* You can buy nuka bran from Japanese grocery stores or online.

1

PREPARING NUKA DOKO FOR NUKAZUKE

ぬか床の準備

Oh, one tip to use throughout the process – use only one hand to mix the nuka doko and keep the other hand clean. This helps prevent nuka doko going everywhere.

When you finish this step, proceed to step two straight away.

You will need

Basic nuka doko

1 litre (34 fl oz) water
100–150 g (3½–5½ oz) sea salt (10%–15% of nuka weight)
1 kg (2 lb 3 oz) nuka (rice bran)
2 red chillies, seeds removed
2–3 × 5 cm (2 in) squares of dried kombu

Additional ingredients (optional)

20–30 g (¾–1 oz) almond powder for umami, nutrition and richness
15–30 ml (½–1 fl oz) beer for fermentation and yeast activity
a few strips of apple, yuzu and/or persimmon peel for aroma
1–2 pieces dried shiitake for umami
1–2 garlic cloves for preservation and aroma
15 g (½ oz) ginger for preservation and aroma
1–2 pinches of bonito flakes for umami and aroma
15 g (½ oz) koji seasoning for fermentation and umami
4–5 pieces of small dried fish for umami
15 g (½ oz) miso for fermentation and umami
10–20 g (¼–¾ oz) rice koji for umami and sweetness
a few roasted soybeans (whole or powdered) for taste
15–30 ml (½–1 fl oz) sake for preservation and umami
0.3–0.5 g shichimi togarashi for preservation and aroma

1. Bring the water to the boil in a large saucepan and stir in the salt until dissolved. Remove from the heat and allow to cool.
2. Put the nuka in a large clean container (at least 3 litres/101 fl oz is ideal), then add the chilli and your choice of additional ingredients. Pour the cooled, salted water on top and mix everything together using your hand. Tuck the kombu pieces into the nuka doko. Now move on to step two: conditioning the nuka doko.

— *NOTE*: You can halve the ingredients to make a smaller portion, if you like.

CONTINUED →

2 SACRIFICIAL PICKLING

捨て漬け

In this step we are growing microbes to make a nice, healthy nuka doko by adding vegetables. This fermentation process, which takes about 2–3 weeks, is important to bring a good flavour to your nuka doko. You can use vegetable scraps for this step: skins, bits off the top and bottom, the outer leaves of wombok and cabbage. I also use the leaves of root vegetables (such as daikon, turnip, carrot etc.).

You will need

4 × 200 g (7 oz) vegetable scraps, such as the outer leaves of wombok (Chinese cabbage), vegetable peels, and daikon, radish and carrot leaves and root tips

1 × quantity basic Nuka doko (see page 189)

1. **Day 1:** Add 200 g (7 oz) of vegetable scraps to the freshly made nuka doko. Mix them in well with your hand. Flatten the surface of the paste with your hand and wipe the container clean. (Keeping the container clean is important.) Place a lid on top.
2. **Day 2:** Mix the nuka doko by putting your hand to the bottom of the container and bringing the bottom part of the nuka to the top; the top part of the nuka will move to the lower part of the container. Flatten the surface of the paste with your hand, then replace the lid.
3. **Day 3:** Repeat what you did on day 2.
4. **Day 4:** Remove the vegetable scraps from the nuka doko. Squeeze the vegetable scraps onto the nuka doko so that the juice is incorporated, then discard the scraps. (The juice and enzymes from the vegetable scraps contribute to the nuka doko fermentation.) Add 200 g (7 oz) more fresh vegetable scraps and mix them with the nuka doko as on day 1.
5. Repeat the process from days 1 to 4 three or four times. Your nuka doko should be ready to pickle with after 2–3 weeks. At this stage, your nuka doko is still young, but some good flavours should have developed. Once you start pickling every day (step 3), your nuka doko flavour will develop even more.

— *NOTE*: Remember, mixing doesn't mean stirring. Nuka doko paste has to move from the bottom to the top and from the top to the bottom. Different types of microbes will live in the top, middle and bottom parts of the nuka doko. It's important to change the location of the microbes to get a good balance.

3 START FERMENTING (FINALLY!)

本漬け

Your nuka doko is now ready to use. So long as you keep using and maintaining this nuka doko, it will last a very, very long time. I hope you can pass it to the next generation in your family.

So, what can we ferment? Seasonal vegetables are the best but any vegetables will work. The vegetables you can eat raw, you can ferment as raw; the vegetables you would normally cook before eating, like potato, cook (boil or steam) before putting into the nuka doko. Try different vegetables and find your favourites. You can ferment a few different types of vegetables at a time, as long as the vegetables are covered in nuka doko. For instance, for my daily nukazuke fermenting I use one cucumber, one orange carrot and one yellow carrot. Sometimes I use more, sometimes less.

When preparing vegetables for fermenting, some vegetables require pre-treatment to remove any bitterness or harshness or to keep the nice colour before fermenting.

Yoko's guide to fermenting with nuka doko

1. Ferment as they are – turnips and carrots. Any types of vegetables that are yummy raw can simply be rinsed, drained and added straight to the nuka doko. I also do this with cauliflower and cabbage. Cut bigger vegetables in halves or quarters, or leave whole and ferment them for longer.
2. Rub with salt – eggplants (aubergines), red radishes, leafy greens and cucumbers. Any vegetables that have bitterness or harshness are best rubbed well with salt, then added to the nuka doko.
3. Steam or cook – potato, pumpkin (winter squash), sweet potato and broccoli. These types of vegetables can be lightly steamed or boiled, then cooled and added to the nuka doko.
4. Sun-dried – daikon, mushrooms and wombok (Chinese cabbage). These types of vegetables can be sun-dried for ½–1 day before being added to the nuka doko, to increase their umami flavour and nutritional value.

CONTINUED →

4

HOW LONG SHOULD WE FERMENT IT FOR?

おいしく漬かるまでどのくらい？

The fermentation time varies depending on the vegetables used and how they are prepared, as well as the room temperature where your nuka doko is kept. Hard vegetables take longer than soft vegetables and large pieces will take longer than small pieces. The moisture content of the vegetables and whether the skin is peeled will also have an effect. If your house is cold, fermentation goes slowly. If it is warm, then the vegetables will be fermented quite quickly.

And! You might like lightly pickled flavours; others might like longer-pickled flavours. There are so many factors involved that I can't predict an exact fermentation time – it can be roughly anywhere from 4 hours to 2 days. What I can say is, if you want a quick ferment, peel the skin and cut the vegetables in half or quarters. If you don't mind taking things slowly, ferment whole vegetables and leave the nuka doko in a cool place. (You can even put it in the refrigerator, as long as you take it out sometimes to warm to room temperature.) Making nukazuke is a case of juggling time and temperature to get the perfect flavour.

And, if it's fermented for a long time, that's okay! There is no rule for how long you should pickle your vegetables. Nukazuke is categorised by the following:

Asazuke
浅漬け
Lightly pickled

Fukazuke
深漬け
Deeply pickled

Furuzuke
古漬け
Aged pickles

As you've probably noticed, these names are used for other pickles as well, not just nukazuke.

— *NOTE*: Making nukazuke is like having a silent conversation with your nuka doko. Although it doesn't speak in words, it communicates through the flavour and aroma of the pickles. You might find yourself asking: is the temperature too warm? Does it need more nutrients to thrive? Maybe it seems a bit upset – could it need a little more salt? By using your senses – sight, smell, taste, touch and even intuition – you can understand what your nuka doko needs and create an environment where it can stay healthy and vibrant. It will reward you with yummy nukazuke.

CONTINUED →

GREAT FRUITS & VEGETABLES FOR NUKAZUKE

APPLE/PERSIMMON

Fruits can be delicious for nukazuke. The combination of the nuka flavour, with its sourness, and the sweetness from the fruit is addictive. I like to pickle apple and persimmon. Choose crispy fruit (especially persimmons, don't pick the soft ones!) and pickle them with their skin on. Cut in half, depending on their size.

AVOCADO

It's important to choose the right firmness when pickling avocado. It should be firm but creamy. Cut the avocado in half, remove the stone and peel the skin. It's richness and creaminess makes a very special pickle. There are many fans of avocado nukazuke – my sister is one of them.

BELL PEPPER

Bell pepper (capsicum) has sweetness, therefore it works quite well as nukazuke. Its juiciness is great, too. I enjoy the brightness this vegetable adds to the plate.

CARROT

I like to pickle carrots without peeling the skin, but be aware that the skin becomes darker (black) after pickling. If you want a nice colour, peel the skin. Orange, red, yellow and purple carrots are all fun to pickle. Carrot is a hard vegetable, so it takes longer to pickle compared to cucumber or turnip, unless you pickle smaller Dutch carrots.

CAULIFLOWER

I pickle raw cauliflower as I enjoy its crunchiness. You can lightly boil or steam it before pickling, but make sure you don't cook it too long. Break it into small, bite-sized florets. Be careful not to cut into the buds, as this can cause the florets to fall apart. I place the florets in a small cotton bag – it's much easier than trying to find all the pieces!

CELERY

Remove the hard strings from the celery before pickling. If pickled for too long, celery tends to become stringy, so light pickling is my recommendation. You can enjoy the unique freshness of celery.

CONTINUED →

CUCUMBER

Cucumbers are the quintessential summer vegetable for nukazuke. Try pickling fresh, newly harvested cucumbers if you can. Cut off both ends, rub them well with salt and put them straight into the nuka doko, whole or halved. They pickle fairly quickly. If you peel some of the skin and put them in the nuka doko in the morning they'll be ready by lunchtime. If you put them in the nuka doko in the afternoon they'll be ready by dinner.

GREEN LEAVES (MIZUNA, BOK CHOY, RADISH LEAVES, ETC.)

Rub salt into the leaves, then add them to the nuka doko. I like both lightly pickled leaves, which you can enjoy for their crispy texture, and furuzuke (aged pickled leaves), which are great in stir-fries or fried rice.

MUSHROOM

I like to sun-dry mushrooms for ½–1 day before adding them to the nuka doko. The moisture of the mushrooms evaporates, concentrating their umami and significantly enhancing their flavour. Tear the sun-dried mushrooms into bite-sized pieces and place them in a cotton bag to prevent them getting scattered in the nuka doko. Pearl oyster, king oyster, shimeji, enoki and fresh shiitake all work very well. You can eat the pickles as is, but I like to quickly pan-fry them – no seasoning required. Sooo yummy.

POTATO

I am not a big fan of potato normally, but I love nukazuke potato. It's amazing how the potato flavour changes. Cut big potatoes into halves or use whole if they are a reasonable size. Steam them in their skins until soft. I like to use nukazuke potato to make potato salad as it has a nice sourness and umami flavour.

SWEET POTATO

This is one of my favourite nukazuke. The sweetness from the sweet potato and the sourness from the nukazuke works so well. I like to use purple-skinned sweet potato. Choose small sweet potatoes and steam them in their skins until just tender. It makes a great snack.

TOMATO

Choose either cherry tomatoes or regular tomatoes – both work. If using large tomatoes, blanch and peel them before pickling. For cherry or regular tomatoes, pickle them with the skins on but score the bottom of the tomatoes with a sharp knife to allow the flavour to penetrate more easily. You can use many different colours of tomatoes.

TURNIP

The sweetness of turnips with the nuka flavour is a great match. The soft texture also makes this a popular nukazuke. Leave some leafy parts on the turnip so you get some green bits when you eat it. If the turnip is big, cut it in half. Pickle small ones whole. You can slice or cut them into wedges to serve.

NOT JUST VEGETABLES

Nukazuke is not only for vegetables – you can pickle tofu, meat and fish as well. Firm (momen) or lightly firm tofu is suitable for nukazuke tofu. Silken tofu is not suitable as it is too soft. Drain the water from the tofu and wrap it in paper towel and place it on a chopping board. Put a plate or another chopping board on top of the tofu to help extract more water. Allow it to rest for at least 30 minutes before unwrapping the tofu and applying new paper towel. Because tofu is delicate, I take some nuka from the nuka doko and use it to wrap the tofu. I place it in a separate container for 1–2 days. Nuka-pickled tofu has a cheese-like quality: it has sourness, saltiness and umami. It is great. You can enjoy it as is, or mush it and make a nukazuke tofu dip.

You can also ferment meat, squid, prawn (shrimp), sashimi and chicken using your nuka doko. However, avoid putting them directly into your nuka doko. Instead, take some nuka and apply it to the meat or fish. Allow it to rest for at least half a day to a full day. Cook your meat or fish as you normally would.

HOW TO SERVE

Remove the vegetables from the nuka doko and rinse them. Nuka is edible, but it's gritty and has an unpleasant texture. Any vegetables you placed in a cotton bag don't need to be rinsed. Cut your vegetables into 3–4 mm (⅛ in) slices or bite-sized chunks and they are ready to serve.

CONTINUED →

5 HOW TO MAINTAIN NUKA DOKO

ぬか床のお手入れ

It's best to mix your nuka doko every day. If you are pickling something every day it shouldn't be an issue because when you take the vegetables out you can mix it. Make sure you put your hand to the bottom of the container and bring it up. If you have more vegetables to pickle, you can put them in. Flatten the surface of the paste with your hand and replace the lid. This is the cycle of nukazuke life.

The reason we need to mix it is because of the microbes. This might get a bit complicated ... nuka doko contains a type of yeast known as film-forming yeast, which thrives in oxygen-rich environments. It can proliferate and produce ethyl acetate, resulting in a glue-like smell. A smell reminiscent of wet socks indicates an overgrowth of butyric acid bacteria at the bottom of the nuka doko, which dislike oxygen. Thoroughly mixing the nuka doko from the bottom to the top will move the oxygen-loving, film-forming yeast to the oxygen-poor bottom and the oxygen-hating butyric acid bacteria to the surface, making the environment less favourable for these bacteria and controlling their growth. So the point is: mixing your nuka doko every day will keep it happy.

A healthy nuka doko should be well balanced with a natural smell that reflects the fermentation process, similar to the mild sourness of yoghurt or sourdough bread, but with its own unique savoury character. It is pleasantly earthy and slightly tangy. I call it yummy stinky. A well-maintained nuka doko should not smell overly sour, musty or rotten.

If you live in a warm region I recommend keeping your nuka doko in the refrigerator to slow the fermentation process. (Unless you can mix twice a day!) Take the nuka doko out of the refrigerator sometimes (let's say once a week) and let it enjoy room temperature for a few hours. Your nuka doko will appreciate it. If you're mixing your nuka doko every day and it still has a glue-like smell, you can put it in the freezer for a day or so. The smell should reduce after a few days.

If you're pickling every day, the amount of nuka doko in your container will gradually reduce. To replenish it, you'll need:

100 g (3½ oz) nuka (rice bran)
½ teaspoon salt
5 cm (2 in) square of dried kombu (optional)
1 dried chilli (optional)

Combine the nuka and salt in a bowl. Add the kombu and chilli, if desired. Add this new mixture to your existing nuka doko and combine well.

Does it look like your nuka doko has mold on the surface?

If you can see a white film on the surface of your nuka doko, this is acid film-forming yeast. It's not mold and it's a natural part of the fermentation process. When this yeast lives on the surface, it may produce an unpleasant smell, but when it works deeper into the oxygen-free layers of the nuka doko, it contributes to the rich aroma and helps balance the acidity, preventing the pickles from becoming overly sour. If the film is thin, you can simply mix it back into the nuka doko to help maintain its health and flavour. However, if it becomes a thick layer (it will look quite white at this stage), scrape it off the surface with a spoon. If you notice something that looks like mold, and is red, orange, blue or black, it is not welcome mold! You definitely need to get rid of it. Remove 2–3 cm (¾–1¼ in) from the top of the nuka doko. Transfer the remaining nuka doko to a clean bowl. Wash the container well and dry it in the sun. When the container is dry put the nuka doko back in and add some fresh nuka (rice bran) and salt at a ratio of 10:1.

If you don't use nuka doko for a long time ...

Sometimes life gets busy or you want to enjoy long holidays and you can't look after your nuka doko every day. That's okay. Remove any vegetables from the nuka doko, put the nuka doko into a ziplock freezer bag, then place it in the freezer until you are ready to use it again. No pressure.

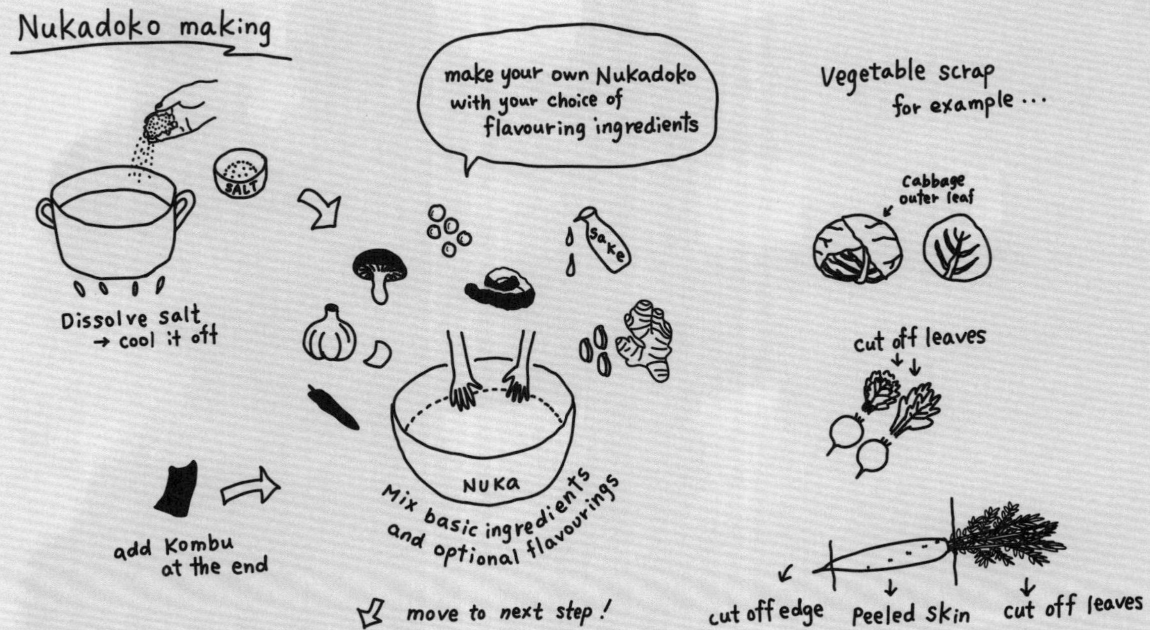
Nukadoko making
make your own Nukadoko with your choice of flavouring ingredients
Vegetable scrap for example ...
SALT
Dissolve salt → cool it off
Sake
Cabbage outer leaf
cut off leaves
NUKA
Mix basic ingredients and optional flavourings
add Kombu at the end
move to next step!
cut off edge
Peeled Skin
cut off leaves

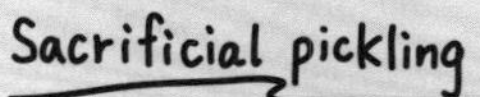
Sacrificial pickling

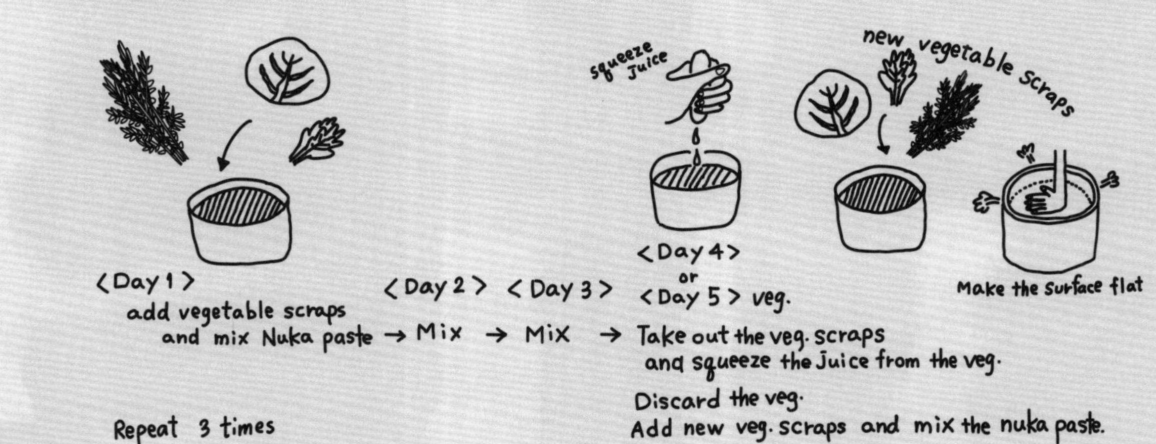
squeeze Juice
new vegetable Scraps
Make the Surface flat
<Day 1>
add vegetable scraps and mix Nuka paste → Mix → Mix →
<Day 2> <Day 3>
<Day 4> or <Day 5> veg.
Take out the veg. scraps and squeeze the Juice from the veg.
Discard the veg.
Add new veg. scraps and mix the nuka paste.
Repeat 3 times

Look after Nukadoko

How to mix Nukadoko

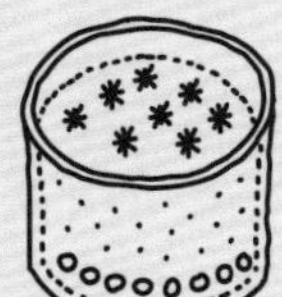

* Film yeast (loves oxygen)
∵ Lactic acid bacteria
o Butyrate-producing bacteria (don't like oxygen)

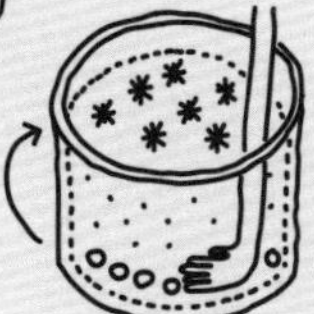

Mix well.

Bottom part comes to the surface.
Surface part moves to the bottom.

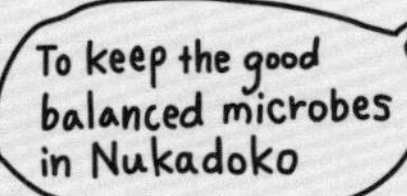

Add some Nuka powder to the Nukadoko

When?!

When the Nukadoko is….

→ Quite wet
→ Less amount
→ Not good smell

TAMARIZUKE

たまり漬け

Tamarizuke are pickles that use tamari, a byproduct from the process of making miso or tamari soy sauce. As miso ferments, a rich liquid surfaces – this is tamari. It's packed with umami, deep flavours and a pleasant sweetness. Known as miso tamari, it's the origin of today's thick, flavourful tamari soy sauce. In a way, it's like a hidden treasure that only those who make miso can fully enjoy.

Traditionally, tamarizuke begins by salting vegetables. Salting helps to concentrate and preserve their natural flavours and aromas, while improving texture. Alternatively, the vegetables can be sun-dried instead of salted. Where I grew up in Japan, autumn to winter was the ideal time for drying vegetables – cold but sunny nearly every day. I remember seeing neighbours with vegetables drying in their gardens. After that, the salted or sun-dried vegetables were soaked in the delicious tamari liquid. This is how tamarizuke are made.

Here in Central Victoria, Australia, where I live, autumn and winter bring misty, rainy days with cloudy skies, so I have to watch the weather carefully and wait for a sunny moment to dry vegetables. (Though, to be honest, I've had my fair share of 'Oh no!' moments with the unreliable weather forecasts.) Even though sun-drying vegetables during autumn and winter isn't as easy as it was when I lived in Japan, I still make the effort because tamarizuke made with sun-dried vegetables is incredibly delicious.

Since I make my own miso, I have access to miso tamari. However, I understand that not everyone makes miso at home. If you don't have miso tamari, you can use soy sauce or tamari soy sauce to make these pickles. I've also included a few quick, modern versions of tamarizuke that don't require salting or drying vegetables, so even busy people can enjoy the rich flavours.

MASTER DAIKON

大根の殿様漬け

PICKLING TIME: *4½ hours*

You will need
1 kg (2 lb 3 oz) daikon
½ red chilli

Pickling liquid
250 ml (8½ fl oz) tamari or soy sauce
100 ml (3½ fl oz) vinegar
150–200 g (5½–7 oz) sugar

STORAGE: *Store in the refrigerator for up to 1 month.*

This is our family's classic winter pickle. I find it so peaceful to see the sliced daikon lined up, drying on the balcony or in the garden. You can buy daikon throughout the year, but winter daikon is definitely the best. It has more sweetness and is less peppery.

This recipe requires you to dry the daikon. This extra step results in a great texture ... and the typical pickled daikon sound when you are eating it. When daikon is dried it shrinks significantly, and since this pickle has a long shelf life, it's perfectly fine to make a large batch. (My family's smallest batch is 5 kg/11 lb of daikon!)

Eat this pickled daikon alongside a meal or serve it with tea and some sweets. Savoury and sweet together is the best.

1. To prepare the daikon, slice it into rounds about 2–3 mm (⅛ in) thick, then slice the rounds into half-moons or quarters. On a sunny day, lay the slices on a zaru (flat bamboo basket) or in a colander and dry outside for ½–1 day, depending on the weather. (The goal is to dry the outer layer but retain some moisture inside. The texture should be floppy, not crunchy.)
2. Place the daikon in a clean container. Remove the seeds from the chilli, then finely slice it.
3. To make the pickling liquid, combine the pickling ingredients and chilli in a saucepan and bring to the boil, stirring, until the sugar has fully dissolved.
4. While the pickling liquid is still hot, pour it over the daikon and mix well to ensure the daikon is fully coated. Place a plate on top to keep the daikon submerged in the liquid. Pop a lid on the container and allow it to rest for 30 minutes.
5. Stir the daikon and pickling mixture, then allow it to rest for a further 4–6 hours, until the flavours have soaked in, before serving.

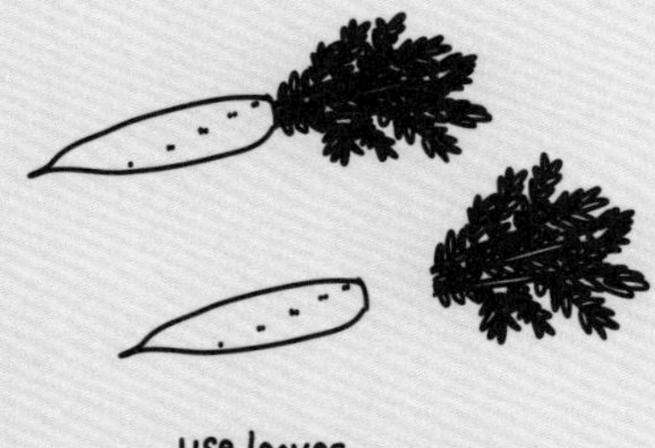

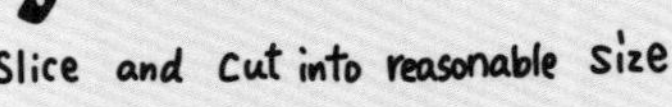

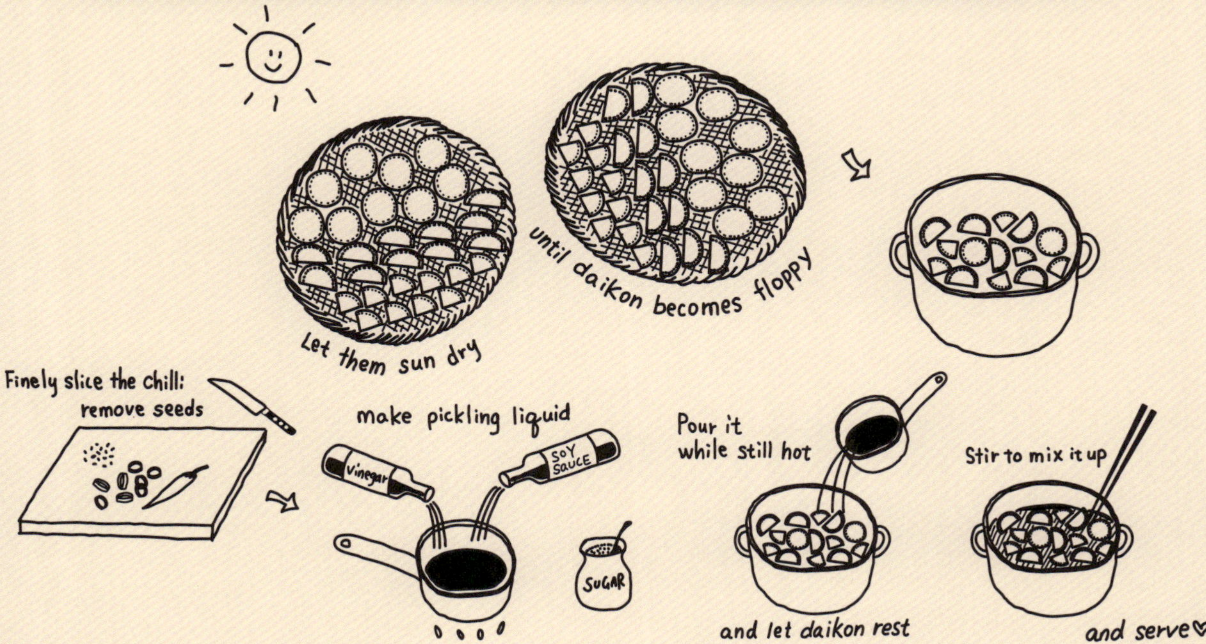
Let them sun dry
until daikon becomes floppy
Finely slice the chill:
remove seeds
make pickling liquid
Vinegar
SOY SAUCE
SUGAR
Pour it
while still hot
and let daikon rest
Stir to mix it up
and serve♡

ONION TAMARIZUKE

玉ねぎのたまり漬け

PICKLING TIME: *4 hours*

You will need

1 onion
60 ml (2 fl oz) tamari or soy sauce

STORAGE: *Store in the refrigerator for up to 1 week.*

Sometimes when you're cooking you end up with leftover onions, right? When that happens, I make this quick pickle, which works perfectly as a light, refreshing side dish. It might just be the simplest pickle recipe in this book.

When using brown onions for pickling, it's important to take a few precautions as their raw state can be quite pungent. If it's the season for new onions, you can simply soak them in water to mellow the flavour, but for regular onions outside of that season it's best to blanch them briefly. This helps remove the harshness while still preserving their crisp texture.

Additionally, when making such a simple pickle, the quality of the ingredients becomes key. Be sure to choose a good-quality traditionally brewed soy sauce or tamari. Check the ingredients list and opt for one without unnecessary additives.

This pickle works well served on tofu or as a noodle topping.

1. Peel the onion and cut it into bite-sized pieces, slices or wedges.
2. If using a new-season onion, simply soak the onion in water for 10–15 minutes. If using a regular onion, blanch it in boiling water for 10 seconds. Drain.
3. Place the onion in a clean container, then pour the tamari on top. Give it a quick stir to make sure all the onion is covered, then pop on a lid.
4. Allow the onion to rest in the refrigerator for at least 4 hours before serving.

OR

OR

PORI-PORI CUCUMBER

ポリポリきゅうり

PICKLING TIME: *1 day*

You will need

1 kg (2 lb 3 oz) cucumbers

Pickling liquid

180 ml (6 fl oz) tamari or soy sauce

180 ml (6 fl oz) vinegar

100 ml (3½ fl oz) mirin

150 g (5½ oz) sugar

30 g (1 oz) ginger, finely sliced (and peeled if you'd prefer)

1–2 red chillies, seeds removed and finely sliced

STORAGE: *Store in the refrigerator for up to 3 weeks.*

Every summer we grow lots of cucumbers in the garden – we end up harvesting mountains of them every day. Our family's challenge is keeping up with the bounty of cucumbers. (It's a happy problem to have!) We enjoy some fresh (with miso – the best), some are turned into nukazuke (see page 196), some are used as asazuke (see pages 76, 82, 84 and 88), and others are made into preserves. This recipe is a preserve that we make every year.

Even though it's a preserve, the freshness of the cucumber is still key. Choose slender cucumbers for the best texture, avoiding the chubbier ones, if possible. The sound we associate with this pickle is 'pori-pori' – a sort of crunchy bite. To achieve that satisfying crunch, remember not to let the cucumbers boil. We want them to absorb the flavour, but we don't want to cook them through completely.

1. Slice the cucumbers into 1–1.5 cm (½ in) rounds.
2. To make the pickling liquid, combine all the ingredients in a large saucepan and bring to the boil, stirring, until the sugar has fully dissolved.
3. Turn the heat off and add the cucumbers. Turn the heat back on to medium. As soon as you see bubbles appear on the surface, turn the heat off again. Do not let it boil. Cover the pan and remove it from the stovetop (to avoid residual heat). Let it sit for 6–8 hours.
4. Pour the cucumber mixture into a colander set over a saucepan to collect the pickling liquid. Bring the pickling liquid to the boil again, then turn the heat off and add the cucumbers back in. Turn the heat back on to medium. When small bubbles start to appear and the cucumbers begin to move, turn the heat off. Do not let it boil. Put a lid on the pan and remove it from the stovetop (to avoid residual heat). Let it sit for 6–8 hours.
5. Repeat the process of boiling and cooling three to four times. The more repetitions, the stronger the flavour.
6. Transfer to a clean container and store in the refrigerator.

— *NOTE:* Even if the broth seems insufficient at first, the cucumbers will release water as you repeat the process, so it will become just right. Be careful not to let it boil or the cucumbers will lose their crunchiness. I do this process four times: morning, noon, night and the next morning – then the pori-pori cucumber is ready to eat.

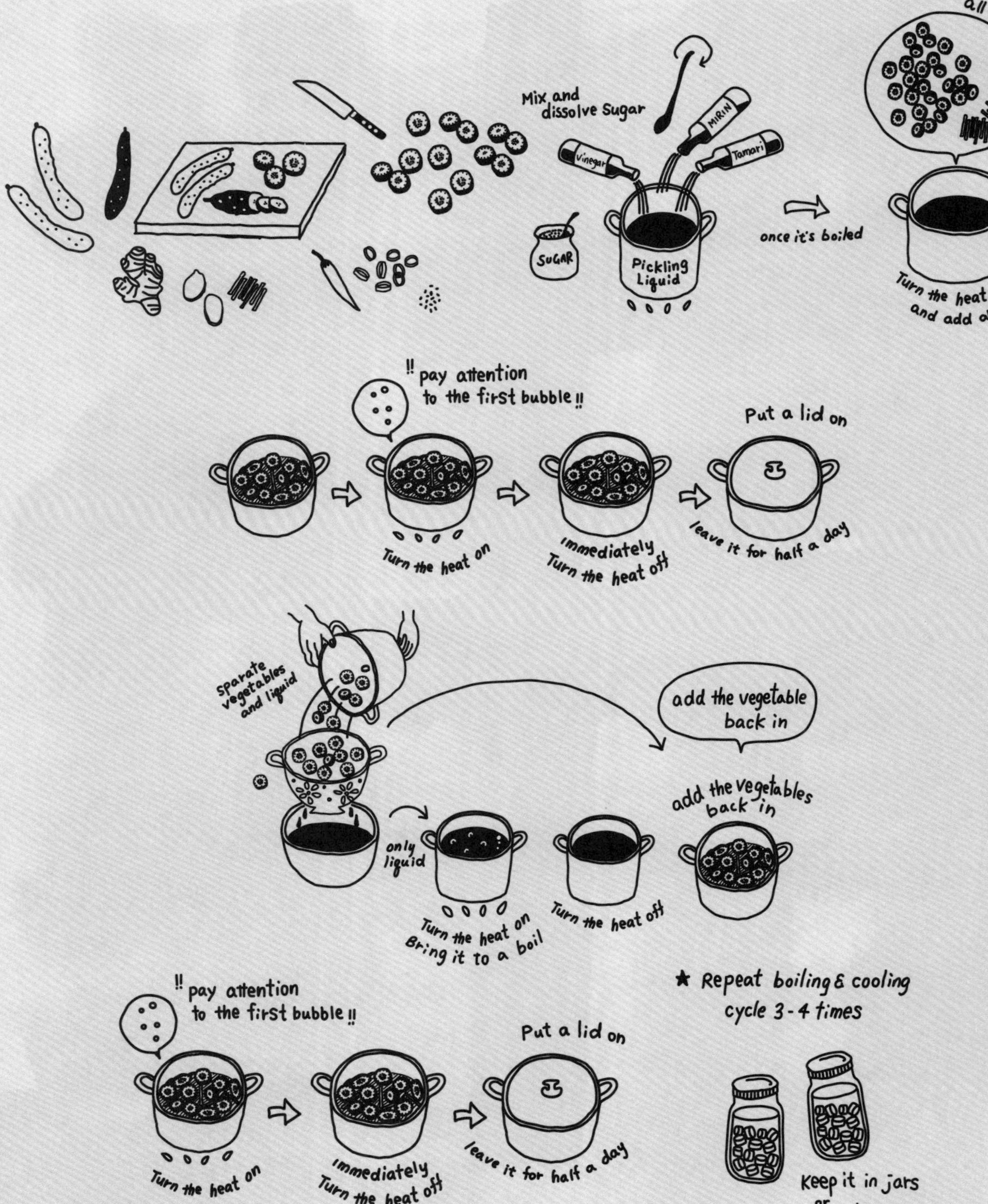
Mix and dissolve Sugar
Vinegar
MIRIN
Tamari
SUGAR
Pickling Liquid
once it's boiled
all in !!
Turn the heat off and add all vegetables
!! pay attention to the first bubble !!
Turn the heat on
immediately Turn the heat off
Put a lid on
leave it for half a day
sparate vegetables and liquid
add the vegetable back in
only liquid
Turn the heat on Bring it to a boil
Turn the heat off
add the vegetables back in
!! pay attention to the first bubble !!
Turn the heat on
immediately Turn the heat off
Put a lid on
leave it for half a day
★ Repeat boiling & cooling cycle 3-4 times
Keep it in jars or containers

こころに響く
大和言葉

EGG & ONION TAMARIZUKE

卵と玉ねぎのたまり漬け

PICKLING TIME: *overnight*

You will need

6 eggs (300 g/10½ oz) or silken or slightly firm tofu

To serve (optional)

green shiso leaves, whole or sliced
bonito flakes
shredded dried chilli

Pickling liquid

50 ml (1¾ fl oz) tamari or soy sauce
15 ml (½ fl oz) sake
5 ml sesame oil
15 ml (½ fl oz) vinegar
10 ml dashi
10–15 g sugar
½ onion
1 spring onion (scallion)
1 garlic clove from Garlic tamarizuke (see page 216) or regular garlic clove, grated
5 g toasted sesame seeds
pinch of salt

STORAGE: *Store in the refrigerator for up to 3 days if the eggs are soft-boiled or 5–6 days if hard-boiled (or if you use tofu).*

When we think of pickles, we usually imagine vegetable pickles. So I'm not sure if eggs can be considered 'pickles' in the traditional sense, but since I enjoy these eggs and onion very much, I wanted to include this recipe in the book. The pickled onion and spring onions bring a wonderful balance to the tamari soy sauce, adding delightful flavours and textures, and the eggs (or tofu) seem very happy in the sauce. I think this is a great little dish to pair with alcohol, or added to a bowl of rice to enjoy in a very Japanese way. They're great as a ramen topping, too.

1. Boil the eggs to your liking. (For this pickle, I prefer jammy eggs, so I cook them for about 8 minutes.) As soon as the eggs are cooked, cool them under running water. When they are cool, peel the shells. If you're using tofu, cut it into 4–6 pieces.
2. To make the pickling liquid, combine the tamari, sake, sesame oil, vinegar, dashi and sugar in a clean container that can hold the eggs or tofu. Stir until the sugar has dissolved.
3. Put the kettle on. While waiting for it to boil, finely chop the onion and spring onion. Put them into a fine mesh sieve then pour the just-boiled water over them.
4. Add the onion and spring onion to the pickling liquid. Add the grated garlic, toasted sesame seeds and pinch of salt. The pickling liquid is now ready.
5. Place the eggs (or tofu) in the pickling liquid. Swirl the pickling liquid around to make sure it covers all of the eggs (or tofu).
6. Pop a lid on the container and allow it to rest in the refrigerator overnight before serving.
7. Cut the eggs in half and serve on shiso leaves, topped with bonito flakes and shredded chilli, if desired. Spoon over a little of the pickling liquid and enjoy.

— *NOTE*: During the pickling period, turn the eggs over occasionally or swirl some liquid over them.

Prepare boiled eggs
cool them
peel the shells
Prepare pickling liquid
DASHI
Vinegar
Tamari
Sesame OIL
SUGAR
SAKE
SALT
sesame seeds
OR
If Tamarizuke garlic, just chop
OR
sometimes Turn it over
put some liquid over egg

GARLIC TAMARIZUKE

にんにくのたまり漬け

PICKLING TIME: *1 month*

You will need
garlic cloves, as many as you like
tamari or soy sauce, enough to cover the garlic

STORAGE: *Store in the pantry for up to 3 years.*

Pickled garlic in tamari. Very simple. Super useful.

Garlic is one of the 'no problem' vegetables in our winter garden. Garlic, broad (fava) beans and daikon. It seems they like our soil. Every year, some of the garlic becomes my signature garlic miso, some gets turned into black garlic and some is used to make this pickled garlic. (For more garlic ideas, see pages 164 and 185.)

The liquid from the pickle will have a beautiful aroma that will gradually turn into an amazing garlic-flavoured tamari. This can be used anytime you want soy sauce and garlic together. (Fried rice? Yes! So yummy with this sauce.) We add it to pasta, too.

It might take some courage, but please try eating the garlic as it is (raw). Once it is pickled nicely, the pungent compounds of the garlic are gone and it becomes a very mellow and delicious pickle. You can eat it as it is, but it's also tasty when chopped and mixed into dressings or blended with cream cheese for a fantastic treat on crackers. You can slice it and use it as a topping as well. Of course, you can use it for cooking. I often enjoy it as a garnish on top of tofu.

I tend to use the tamari much more quickly than the garlic, so each time the tamari runs low, I simply top it up with fresh tamari while leaving the garlic as it is. It still works.

1. Peel the garlic cloves.
2. Put the cloves in a jar.
3. Pour the tamari into the jar, completely covering the garlic and keep it in the pantry.
4. You can use the liquid straight away. The garlic is ready to use when it starts to take on the tamari colour.

NAMETAKE

なめたけ

PICKLING TIME: *3 hours*

You will need
200 g (7 oz) enoki mushrooms

Pickling liquid
30 ml (1 fl oz) tamari or soy sauce
40 ml (1¼ fl oz) mirin
10 ml sake
5 g ginger, finely sliced

STORAGE: *Store in the refrigerator for up to 1 week.*

This was my absolute favourite pickle when I was little. I used to put it on rice, tofu or grated daikon, making it a breakfast staple. I think the combination of the sweet flavour and the umami from the mushroom was a real treat for a child. I also liked the texture.

Now that I've grown up, I've gradually come to prefer savoury over sweet, so this seasoning is less sweet than the pickles I enjoyed when I was young. I also enjoy the slippery texture of this pickle. I wonder if I can make it with pine mushrooms? It is going to be next year's project.

1. Trim and discard the base from the enoki mushrooms. Cut the mushrooms into 2–3 cm (¾–1¼ in) lengths and separate them.
2. Mix the pickling ingredients in a saucepan, then add the enoki mushrooms. Bring to the boil over medium heat, then cover with a lid, reduce the heat to low and simmer for 5–6 minutes. Remove the pan from the heat, give the mushrooms a stir and allow to cool.
3. Place the mushrooms and liquid in a jar. Pop on the lid and allow it to rest in the refrigerator for 3 hours before serving.

— *NOTE*: I also like to use this pickle as a sauce. Sometimes I mix it with sliced Garlic tamarizuke (see page 216) to make a sauce to serve with meatloaf. I also make a sauce by combining nametake with Umeboshi (see page 269) for a fresh, ume-flavoured version. When I do that I use less tamari and more sake to enhance the ume.

SHISO SEED POD TAMARIZUKE

紫蘇の実のたまり漬け

PICKLING TIME: *2 days*

You will need

80 g (2¾ oz) green shiso seed pods

Pickling liquid

80 ml (2½ fl oz) tamari or soy sauce

20 ml (¾ fl oz) mirin (if you use soy sauce, increase the mirin to 40 ml/1¼ fl oz)

8 g ginger, finely sliced

STORAGE: *Store in the refrigerator for up to 6 months.*

– *NOTE:* Shiso seed pods are still immature when the plant is in full bloom – at this stage they lack the characteristic popping texture. However, if they are left to mature too much, the outer skin becomes tough. The best time to harvest shiso seed pods is right before the flowers finish blooming – when there are only two or three flowers remaining at the tip of the stalk. This is when you get both perfect texture and flavour.

Shiso, also known as Japanese basil or green/red perilla, is becoming quite popular to grow in the garden and many people ask me how to use it. Both red and green shiso are commonly used in Japanese cuisine. They are herbs, so mainly they are used as a garnish or made into a paste. I make shiso cordial as well, which is very popular at my market stall. The seed pods of shiso (shiso no mi) are often served with sashimi for presentation, but they are also used as a garnish with wasabi. The popping texture ('puchi-puchi' in Japanese) enhances the fresh aroma of shiso. Collecting shiso seeds and preserving them as salted pickles or tamari pickles is very convenient. I always have some in my refrigerator and I enjoy them on rice, with tofu, or whenever I want to feel the taste and aroma of Japan. You can also add them to other preserves such as fukujinzuke (see page 223) or furikake (see page 80).

1. To harvest the shiso seed pods, hold the tip of the shiso spike with one hand and use the fingers of your other hand to strip the seeds from top to bottom. (I really like this feeling!) If you grow shiso at home, one to two plants will yield enough seed pods.
2. Place the seed pods in a bowl of water and rinse them well. Drain into a fine mesh sieve.
3. To make the pickling liquid, combine the ingredients in a saucepan and bring to the boil. Turn the heat off and allow the liquid to cool.
4. Fill a bowl with water and add a few ice cubes. Blanch the shiso seed pods in boiling water for 15–20 seconds, then immediately plunge them into the iced water. Leave them for 1–2 minutes.
5. Drain the seed pods, then squeeze them to remove the excess liquid.
6. Place the seed pods in a clean jar and pour the pickling liquid on top. Give it a stir, then pop the lid on.
7. Allow the seed pods to rest in the refrigerator for at least 2 days before serving.

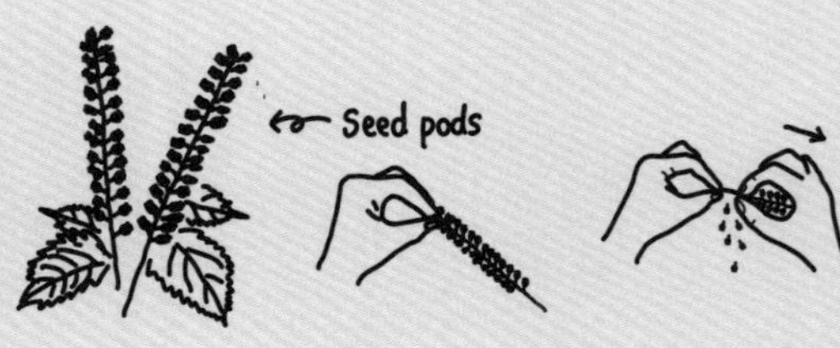

Rinse!
Quickly blanch
15-20 sec.
COOL it off
Cold water
Squeeze out water
MIRIN
Tamari
COOL it off
Pour it in
Ready in 2 days

FUKUJINZUKE

福神漬け

PICKLING TIME: *overnight*

You will need

150 g (5½ oz) daikon
100 g (3½ oz) lotus root
100 g (3½ oz) eggplant (aubergine)
100 g (3½ oz) Japanese or Lebanese cucumbers
50 g (1¾ oz) young broad (fava) bean pods
20 g (¾ oz) ginger, sliced into 2–3 cm (¾–1¼ in) long strips
15 g (½ oz) shiso seed pods
5 g salt

Pickling liquid

100 ml (3½ fl oz) tamari or soy sauce
100 ml (3½ fl oz) mirin
30 g (1 oz) sugar
20 ml (¾ fl oz) vinegar
5 cm (2 in) square of dried kombu, finely sliced

STORAGE: *Store in the refrigerator for up to 2 months.*

This sweet and salty pickle is traditionally served with Japanese curry. But, of course, it's just as delicious when enjoyed on its own or with other meals.

The fun part of making this pickle is that you get to choose seven different vegetables yourself. Try making it a few times with different combinations to find your perfect version of fukujinzuke.

1. Cut the daikon into thin, fan-shaped slices about 3–4 mm thick. Spread the slices on a zaru (flat bamboo basket) or in a colander and dry them in the sun for 4–6 hours to enhance their texture. For the lotus root, peel the skin and slice it into fan-shaped pieces. Soak them in water for 5 minutes, then drain. For the eggplant, peel the skin, cut the flesh into small pieces, then soak it in water for 5 minutes and drain. Cut the cucumber into thin slices.
2. Combine the daikon, lotus root, eggplant, cucumber, broad bean pods, ginger and shiso seed pods in a large bowl, add the salt and mix well. Let it sit for 20–30 minutes, then squeeze the vegetables firmly with both hands to remove the excess water.
3. To make the pickling liquid, combine all the ingredients in a saucepan and bring to the boil. When it begins to boil, add the vegetables. As soon as it boils again – this should take about 15 seconds – remove it from the heat. This method will ensure a nice, crisp texture. If you prefer a softer texture, you can let the vegetables simmer for up to 1 minute.
4. Pour the vegetables into a colander set over a saucepan to collect the liquid. Bring the liquid to a simmer over medium heat and cook for 5–6 minutes.
5. Place the vegetables in a clean container or jar and pour the hot pickling liquid over the vegetables, covering them completely. Allow the liquid to cool, then pop on a lid.
6. Allow it to rest overnight before serving.

— *NOTE*: You can also use the following vegetables: bamboo shoots, carrot, green shiso leaves and shiitake mushrooms.

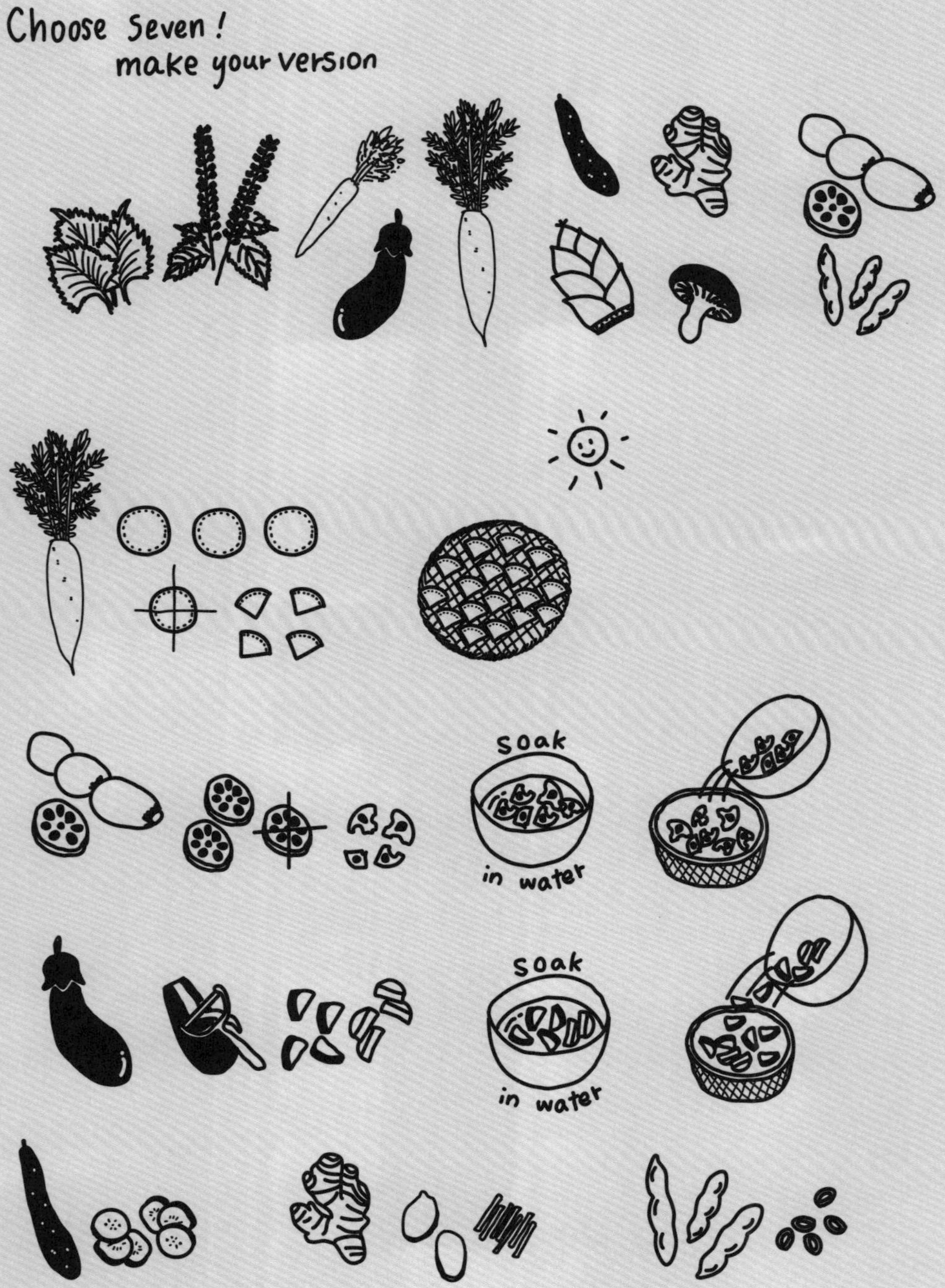

Choose seven!
make your version

soak
in water

soak
in water

What a happy collaboration
all seven go in
squeeze out water
Prepare pickling liquid
Vinegar
Tamari
SUGAR
MIRIN
add veggies in
Bring it to a boil
as soon as it boils again
Remove from the heat
Simmer for 5-6 min.
pour over the hot pickling liquid

MIXED MUSHROOM TAMARIZUKE

色々きのこのたまり漬け

PICKLING TIME: *3 hours*

You will need

500 g (1 lb 2 oz) mixed mushrooms of your choice, such as shimeji, oyster, pearl oyster, shiitake, enoki, pine, slippery jacks or yellow mushrooms

2 Garlic tamarizuke cloves (see page 216) or regular garlic cloves (optional)

5 g pink peppercorns, to serve (optional)

Pickling liquid

50 ml (1 ¾ fl oz) tamari or soy sauce

50 ml (1 ¾ fl oz) mirin

20 ml (¾ fl oz) vinegar

pinch of salt

½–1 red chilli, seeds removed, finely sliced

10 ml sesame oil or olive oil (or half and half)

STORAGE: *Store in the refrigerator for up to 2 weeks.*

When I lived in Tokyo, I used to attend a seasonal vegetable cooking class in Sendagi. The amazing part of this cooking class was that we could access organically grown vegetables, including mushrooms. I learned about many types of mushrooms and since then I've enjoyed mixing different varieties in my cooking.

This pickle celebrates autumn. It's similar to the nametake on page 218, but this one gives you different textures and flavours from each mushroom. And apparently, when more than three kinds of mushrooms are combined, the umami will be enhanced. The diversity and collaboration of mushrooms is amazing, isn't it?

This tamarizuke is delicious on baguettes or udon noodles. It also works well as a simple appetiser – just place a small amount on crackers and serve it as a finger food.

1. Remove and discard the stems from all of the mushrooms. Tear or cut the mushrooms into bite-sized pieces.
2. Bring a large saucepan of water to the boil, then add the mushrooms. Allow the water to boil again for 30 seconds, then drain the mushrooms onto a zaru (flat bamboo basket) or in a colander. Allow the mushrooms to cool.
3. To make the pickling liquid, combine the ingredients in a bowl.
4. Place the mushrooms in a clean container, add the pickled garlic and pour the pickling liquid over the top. Stir to combine everything and pop on a lid.
5. Allow it to rest for at least 3 hours before serving. I like to sprinkle over a few pink peppercorns for colour and flavour.

— *NOTE*: I usually use rice vinegar or apple cider vinegar when I make this pickle, but it's also delicious when made with balsamic vinegar.

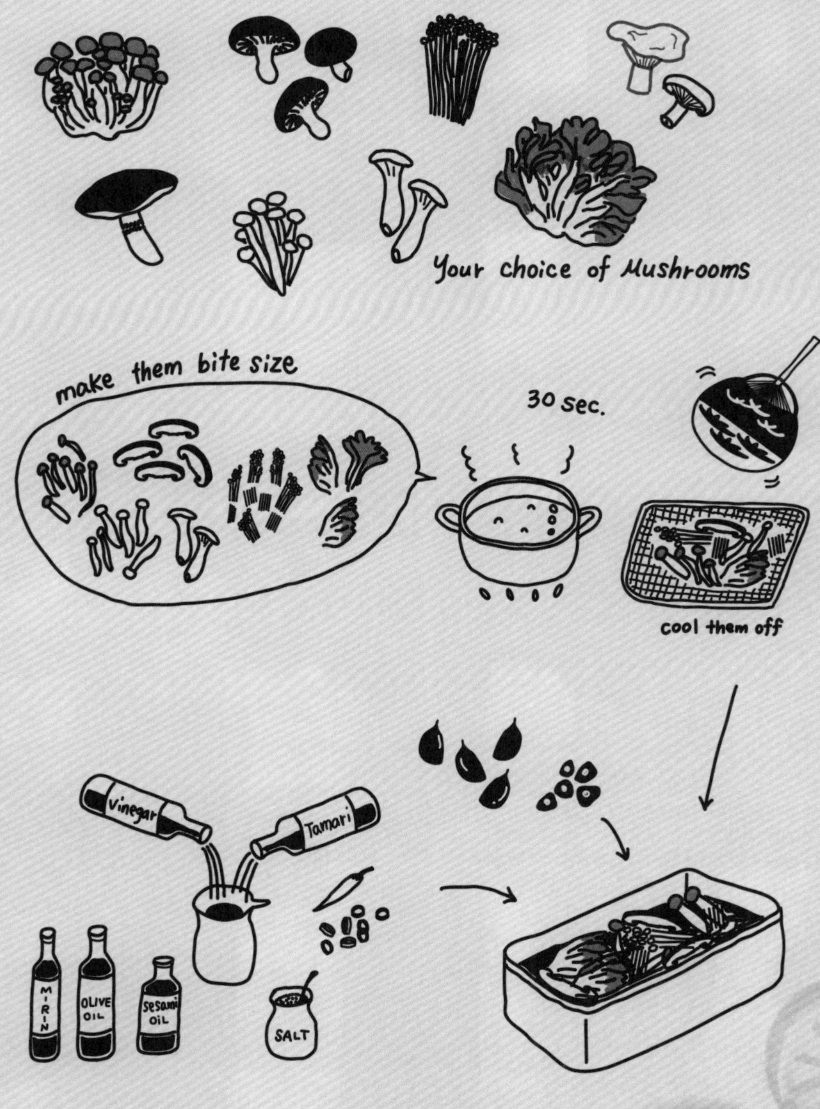
Your choice of Mushrooms
make them bite size
30 sec.
cool them off
Vinegar
Tamari
MIRIN
OLIVE OIL
sesami OIL
SALT

CLASSIC OTSUKEMONO

昔ながらのお漬物

When I was younger, whenever we went to visit friends or relatives my parents would be served green tea, rice crackers and otsukemono. Sometimes the children were served small sweets, but the adults were always gathered around the pickles, chatting. Instead of biscuits or cake, the pickles were the treat. After I moved to Melbourne, Australia, I had the opportunity to visit a Japanese woman's house – I forget the exact purpose of the visit – but there were some other Japanese women there and they were having a chat over pickles. The scenes I remembered from my childhood came back. The women had been living in Melbourne for a long time and they told me they were sick of having biscuits and cakes, and also wanted to avoid becoming overweight from eating sweets. So instead, they bring their own homemade pickles to share and enjoy when they gather to chat. It's an awesome idea. They celebrate the seasons and share their pickling knowledge. The pickles are also a great accompaniment to green tea.

Unfortunately, that generation is getting older and not many people make pickles anymore, especially fermented pickles. My family is one of the older-style families who still make a lot of pickles using vegetables grown in their garden, and I've been fortunate to watch and learn from my mum.

In this chapter, I want to share some of the knowledge passed down from my parents' generation. I will introduce traditional pickles that, while a bit time-consuming, are deliciously fermented. Although they take time to make, the resulting taste is exceptional. Even with a busy lifestyle, I think making pickles makes our life and soul richer.

TAKUAN

たくあん

FERMENTATION TIME:
1 month

Takuan is another popular type of Japanese pickle. You've probably seen long, yellow daikon in plastic bags at grocery stores – that's takuan. It's pickled using nuka (rice bran) and it's like nukazuke (see pages 189–197), but the method is a bit different. Nukazuke is made by fermenting raw vegetables in fermented paste (nuka doko), whereas takuan involves sun-drying the vegetables first to remove moisture, then pickling them in a mixture of dried rice bran, salt and chilli. This process requires several months of fermentation with the use of weights (often a big pickling stone). On the other hand, weights are not needed for nukazuke and the pickling period can be short – only a few hours. Despite using similar ingredients, there are various differences, making them distinct in my opinion.

Seeing rows of daikon, leaves intact, basking in the sun to dry is one of the quintessential winter scenes in many areas of Japan. The cold wind and sunshine create the ideal conditions for this process: the daikon becomes much sweeter and nutritionally richer. More than anything, the unique texture and satisfying crunch of takuan comes from this sun-drying method. Additionally, the dietary fibre content nearly doubles compared to raw daikon, and it also provides vitamin D.

However, I understand that this process isn't easy. I struggle to fully dry daikon in Melbourne, as winter here tends to be wet with many misty and rainy days. My daikon often ends up with some black spots on the skin, which isn't ideal, but I still make takuan with them. It works just fine in the end. Alternatively, you can use a food dehydrator (which is different from drying naturally, but still effective) or you can follow the salting method to draw moisture out of the daikon.

Takuan pairs wonderfully with rice. When I pack rice in a bento box, adding a few slices of yellow takuan on the side or atop the rice – perhaps alongside a red umeboshi – it brings me a small but certain happiness.

There are two steps to making takuan. First you must prepare the daikon ...

CONTINUED →

1 SUN-DRYING THE DAIKON

大根を天日で干す

During winter, our clothesline often transforms into a spot for drying daikon radishes. I wonder what my neighbours think when they see it ... I tie several daikon together with rope to hang them. There are two different methods for hanging the daikon, which I'll explain below.

You will need
10 kg (22 lb) slim daikon with leaves
peel of 1 apple (optional)
peel of 1 persimmon (optional)

1. If you don't have slim daikon, cut the daikon in half lengthways.
2. Now choose either method A or method B for hanging the daikon. For method A, you'll need to cut the leaves off the daikon but don't throw them away – you'll use them in the next step. Be sure to dry them along with the daikon. For method B, keep the daikon leaves on.
3. Method A: Grab a ball of kitchen twine and make a loop in the end of the string, paying attention to the direction that the ends overlap (see illustration on page 240). Make another loop to the right of the first one. Now, place the first (left) loop on top of the second (right) loop. Once layered, pass a daikon through the loops and pull tightly to secure it in place. Amazingly, it won't slip out.
4. Next, create another set of two loops in the same way, overlap them, then pass a daikon through and pull tight. Repeat this process for all the daikon you want to dry.
5. You can secure each daikon at one or two points with the string – two points will provide more stability. Don't forget to dry the leaves to use later.
6. Method B: Alternatively, you can leave the leaves attached to the daikon and tie the leaves of two daikon together with string, then hang them over a rod to dry. I often hang them on a clothes hanger.
7. Once all the daikon are securely tied, hang them in a well-ventilated area, protected from rain. (I like to hang daikon, persimmon and wombok together. They look so cute.) As long as it doesn't rain it's a very peaceful scene. But when it looks like rain, things get hectic! I have to bring everything in quickly and then I panic, wondering, 'Where should I hang them?' To avoid this, it's best to dry the

CONTINUED →

daikon in a sheltered space, such as on a balcony with a roof – somewhere with good ventilation that can also keep them safe from the rain. The daikon can take anywhere from 3 days to 2 weeks to dry – it all depends on the weather. You'll know it is ready when you can bend it with both hands into a 'C' or 'U' shape. Additionally, the dried weight should decrease to at least half – possibly even one-third – of its original weight.

8. While you are sun-drying the daikon, you can prepare dried apple or persimmon peels, which are often used to add aroma to the takuan. Peel the fruit and place the peels on a zaru (flat bamboo basket), or similar. Leave them to dry outside in a sheltered place for at least half a day (depending on the weather), until they are either half-dried or fully dried. It's up to you.

— *NOTE*: When daikon is sun-dried, its moisture and pungency are reduced, resulting in a concentrated umami and sweetness. Fortunately, this process also increases the levels of beneficial components like amino acids, glutamic acid and gamma-aminobutyric acid (GABA). By immersing this nutrient-rich daikon in nutritious nuka (the byproduct of milling brown rice into white rice), these nutrients further infuse into the takuan. Additionally, the plant-based lactic acid bacteria naturally present on the daikon feed on the sugars in the rice bran and daikon, multiplying in the process. As the lactic acid bacteria thrive, they inhibit the growth of harmful bacteria, acting as beneficial microorganisms that play a crucial role in the human body. Authentic takuan is truly a treasure trove of health benefits.

2

FERMENTING THE DAIKON

干し大根を漬ける

In the past, people used to pickle daikon in large wooden barrels, but you can use any type of container. Since you'll need to add a weight on top, a tall, straight-sided container or one with a wide opening is easiest to use. Depending on the amount I'm making, I use either an enamel container or a ceramic pot.

Takuan pickles are made using rice bran (nuka). When you first start pickling, the rice bran is in a powdery state, but as the daikon releases moisture (even after all that drying, it still releases water!), it mixes with the rice bran and turns it into a paste-like consistency.

In the past, more salt was used (7–10 per cent), allowing for long-term storage. However, it tends to make the pickles quite salty, so I use a reduced amount of salt (4 per cent). Once the flavour has deepened to my liking, and when the weather becomes warm (e.g. when spring comes), I switch to storing the daikon in the refrigerator. For those making takuan for the first time and feeling unsure, starting with a salt level of 5–6 per cent might be a good idea for peace of mind. As long as the takuan remains in the rice bran, it can last for a long time. The key is deciding which stage of pickling you prefer – it all comes down to personal taste.

In addition to apple and persimmon peel, yuzu peel is also popular to add. Kombu adds umami, while chilli helps to prevent spoilage. If you want your takuan to have a nice yellow colour, add ground turmeric; without it, the pickles will take on a natural hue – somewhere between pale yellow, off-white or a soft, mellow shade of yellow. Either way, it's up to your preference.

You will need
sun-dried daikon
sun-dried daikon leaves
peel of 1 sun-dried apple (optional)
peel of 1 sun-dried persimmon (optional)
peel of 1 yuzu (optional)
5 cm (2 in) square of dried kombu, sliced
whole chillies (1 chilli for every 2 sun-dried daikon)

Pickling mixture
nuka (10% of dried daikon weight)
salt (4% of dried daikon weight)
sugar (0–5% of dried daikon weight)
ground turmeric (0.1% of dried daikon weight; optional)

CONTINUED →

1. Weigh the sun-dried daikon to determine the ratio of pickling ingredients required. If you used method B, cut the leaves off and set them aside before you weigh the daikon.
2. Combine the pickling mixture in a large bowl.
3. Spread a couple of handfuls of the mixture in the base of a large container.
4. Arrange the dried daikon in a single layer, packing them as tightly as possible and leaving no gaps.
5. Cover the first layer of daikon with some of the pickling mixture, then scatter some fruit peel (if using), kombu and chillies on top.
6. Repeat this layering process: pickling mixture + daikon + pickling mixture + fruit peel, kombu and chilli + pickling mixture – until all of the daikon has been used. Finish with the dried daikon leaves.
7. Place an inner lid on top, followed by a weight at least twice as heavy as the dried daikon. Place a lid on top of this. If the weight sticks out from the container and the lid doesn't sit properly, cover the container with a plastic bag and newspaper, securing it tightly to keep out dust and debris.
8. After about 1 month the volume of the daikon will have reduced to about two-thirds and the nuka powder will have become a paste-like consistency. At this point the pickles are ready to eat.
9. Reduce the weight by half and store the pickles as they are. As long as the daikon are in the pickling mixture, they are safe. You can leave them as long as you like – some people like 3-year-old takuan (although more salt is used for long-term storage).
10. To serve, only take the amount of takuan you'd like to eat. Slice and serve as a side dish, or chop into small pieces and use as a topping for tofu or mixed with kimchi. You can also add takuan to fried rice and serve it with raw tuna or even cheese.

STORAGE: *Store in a cool, dark place for up to 3 months during winter. When spring arrives, store it in the refrigerator.*

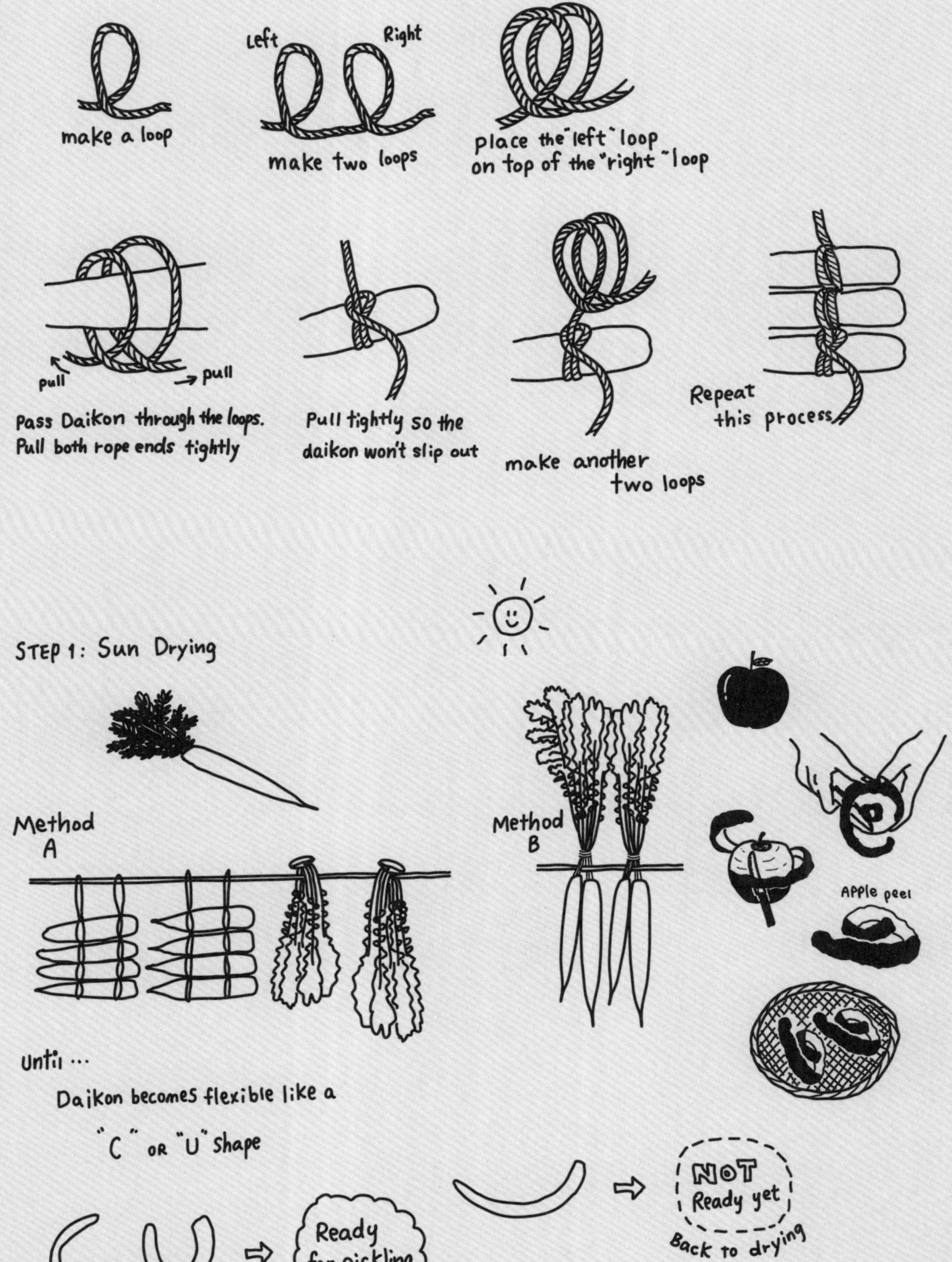
Left
Right
make a loop
make two loops
place the "left" loop
on top of the "right" loop
pull
pull
Pass Daikon through the loops.
Pull both rope ends tightly
Pull tightly so the
daikon won't slip out
make another
two loops
Repeat
this process
STEP 1: Sun Drying
Method
A
Method
B
Apple peel
Until ...
Daikon becomes flexible like a
"C" OR "U" shape
Ready
for pickling
NOT
Ready yet
Back to drying

STEP 2: Pickling
Check
the dried daikon's weight
10%
NuKa
4%
SALT
0~5%
Sugar
0.1%
Turmeric
of dried daikon's weight
Mix all
Cover the layer
with this mixture
Tightly Pack
layer by layer
Aroma & Umami
apple peel
Yuzu skin
Kombu
Chilli
add to each layer
Use daikon leaves
to fill the gaps
Happy
Pickling ♡

KOMBU JIME

昆布締め

FERMENTATION TIME: *5–6 hours*

You will need

dried kombu (enough to sandwich the vegetables)

sake or vinegar, for brushing

vegetables, such as asparagus, bell pepper (capsicum), broccolini, carrot, lotus root, mushrooms, snow peas (mangetout), turnip (including the stems and leaves), zucchini (courgette)

STORAGE: *Store the vegetables only in a clean container in the refrigerator for up to 3 days.*

Kombu jime is a preserving method from the era when refrigeration was not yet advanced. From the mid-Edo era to the Meiji era, a cargo ship called *Kitamaebune* was sent from Hokkaido to Osaka on the Sea of Japan. Hokkaido is famous for kombu, and this kombu jime was developed using their beautiful kombu. By placing fresh ingredients like sashimi between sheets of kombu, the kombu absorbs extra moisture. It helped to keep seafood fresh when refrigeration technology was not yet available.

Nowadays, this method is appreciated for its ability to enhance the flavour of ingredients. We still use this technique for seafood, but vegetables are also used. The sweetness and umami from kombu transfers to the ingredients, bringing a deeper flavour and delightful texture. Simply sandwiched between kombu, this small extra step makes a big difference. It's good with sake, too.

1. I use two 12 × 15 cm (4¾ × 6 in) trays to make kombu jime, but you can use whatever size trays or containers you have. Prepare the kombu by wiping it with sake or vinegar using a cloth or brush to soften it.
2. Slice the vegetables however you prefer them. Set aside any vegetables that you would eat raw.
3. Bring a saucepan of water to the boil and add a pinch of salt. Blanch the remaining vegetables briefly, then transfer them to a zaru (flat bamboo basket) or similar to cool. To speed up the cooling process and retain the vegetables' colour, I like to fan them.
4. Place a layer of kombu on the first tray.
5. Once the vegetables are cool, place both the raw and blanched vegetables on the kombu in a single layer.
6. Cover the vegetables with another layer of kombu, then lay the second tray on top and ensure everything is sealed tightly.
7. Allow the vegetables to rest for half a day to a full day before serving. If you don't finish eating the vegetables all at once, they will become over-pickled if left in the kombu, so store them in a separate container in the refrigerator.

— *NOTES*: You can buy flat kombu or wavy (curly) kombu, but you'll find that flat kombu is easier to use.

You can keep making kombu jime and reuse the kombu two or three times.

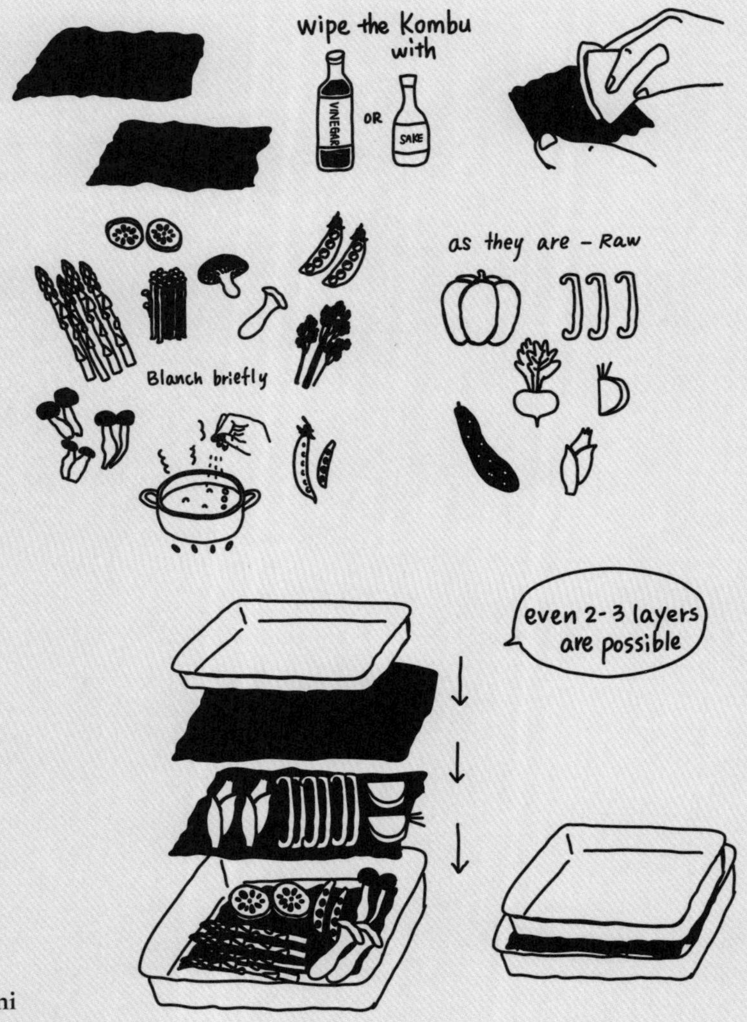

Kombu tsukudani
昆布の佃煮

After using kombu to make kombu jime, I often enjoy making kombu tsukudani to serve with rice or put in onigiri. This way we don't waste food.

Kombu tsukudani is a traditional Japanese condiment made by simmering kombu in soy sauce and mirin or sake until it becomes soft and flavourful, with a sweet and savoury taste.

To make kombu tsukudani, finely slice the kombu into thin strips or squares. Place the kombu in a saucepan with enough water to cover and add 5 ml of vinegar. Bring to a boil, then reduce the heat and simmer for 5–10 minutes, until the kombu becomes soft. Add 15 ml (½ fl oz) each of soy sauce and mirin (and a big pinch of sugar if you like it sweeter) and simmer over medium–low heat until the liquid is fully reduced. To serve, stir through some toasted sesame seeds and enjoy.

SHIBAZUKE

しば漬け

FERMENTATION TIME:
1 week–10 days

You will need

45–100 g (1½–3½ oz) red shiso (10–20% of vegetable weight)

450 g (1 lb) small, thin eggplants (aubergine) and/or Japanese or Lebanese cucumbers

50 g (1¾ oz) myoga (Japanese ginger flower buds) and/or young ginger and/or carrot

salt (4% of vegetable and red shiso weight)

STORAGE: *Store in the refrigerator for up to 1 month.*

This authentic pickle is made by lactic acid fermentation. The method is simple: pickle vegetables with salt and let them ferment. For shibazuke, the most popular vegetable used is eggplant with red shiso (red perilla), but you can also add cucumber, myoga, young ginger and carrot, depending on your preference.

Red shiso is well known for its use in umeboshi or ume drinks. One of its health benefits is rosmarinic acid, which helps alleviate allergy symptoms. Additionally, it has antibacterial and preservative properties, protects mucous membranes and skin and is rich in polyphenols.

Kyoto is a major producer of red shiso, and shibazuke originates from the region. You can make a quick version using umezu, the byproduct from making umeboshi, but here I want to show you the authentic method. I like to see the colour change when I use red or purple vegetables – the colour becomes more vibrant after a few days as the pH levels lower.

The most common and classic way to enjoy shibazuke is with a bowl of plain rice, as the pickle enhances the sweet flavour of the rice. Shibazuke is also a great filling for sushi or onigiri. It pairs particularly well with vinegared rice, balancing the flavours. It's delicious when placed on top of tofu and it's also great in sandwiches, especially ham or cheese. It works well as a tapas and can be added to Japanese-style salads (especially those with daikon, seaweed and cucumber). The versatility of shibazuke makes it easy to pair with almost any dish.

1. Pull the shiso leaves from the stems. Trim the ends of the eggplants, leaving the calyx attached. Cut the eggplants in half lengthways and thinly slice at an angle. Soak the eggplant in a bowl of water for 5–10 minutes (this prevents the cut surface of the eggplants from turning black due to oxidation), while you prepare the other vegetables. Cut the cucumbers in half lengthways and thinly slice them at an angle. If using, cut the myoga lengthways into six pieces and thinly slice the ginger and carrot.
2. Squeeze the water from the eggplant and combine in a bowl with all the other vegetables. Add the salt and mix it through, then allow to rest for 5–6 minutes.

— *NOTE*: Since exposure to the air can cause discolouration, when you take shibazuke out of its container, eat it promptly!

CONTINUED →

3. Use your fingers to gently massage the vegetables for 1–2 minutes. Firmly squeeze the vegetables to remove any excess liquid (which will be bitter) and discard.
4. Place the vegetables in a clean container, followed by an inner lid, then a weight at least twice as heavy as the vegetables. (Weighing down the mixture helps create a deeper flavour as it ferments.) Pop on the outer lid.
5. Unless your home is nice and cool inside even during a hot summer, allow the pickles to rest in the refrigerator for about 1 week, or until they turn a vibrant colour.

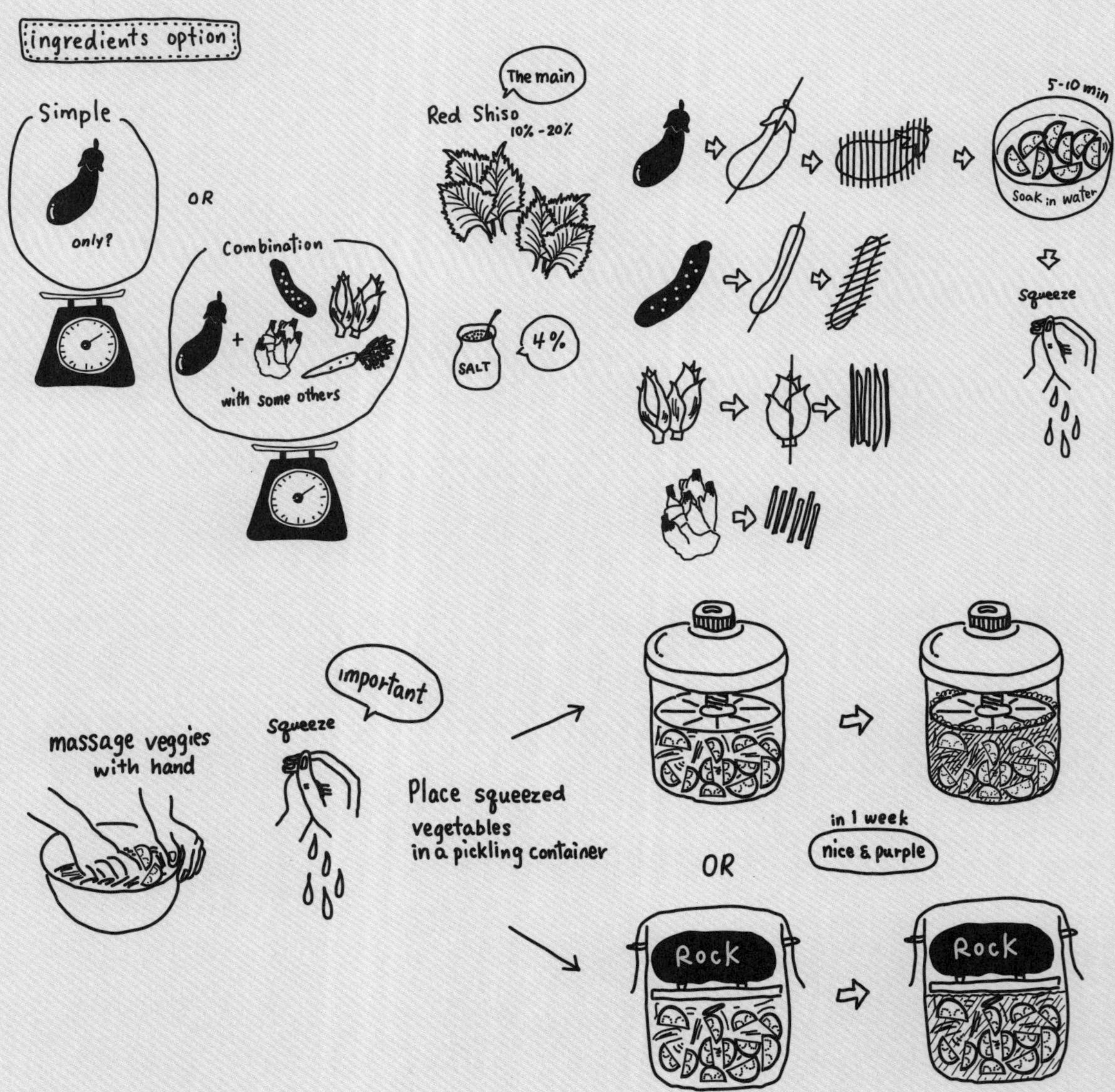

AONA OTUKEMON

青菜のおつけもん

FERMENTATION TIME:
4–5 days or 8–9 days

You will need

500 g (1 lb 2 oz) green leafy vegetables
½ red chilli
5 cm (2 in) square of dried kombu
15 g (½ oz) salt (3% of vegetable weight)

Homemade dashi (optional)

2 g dried kombu or dried mushrooms, or 5 g bonito flakes (a combination of all three is even better)
200 ml (7 fl oz) water

Pickling liquid (optional)

200 ml (7 fl oz) dashi
30 ml (1 fl oz) mirin
15 ml (½ fl oz) sake
4 g salt
3 ml light soy sauce

STORAGE: *Store in the refrigerator for 1 week.*

In Japan, a wealth of leafy greens are used for pickling and each variety is uniquely suited to a different region and climate. For example, some leaves are softened by repeated exposure to snow, while others are grown with the help of fresh spring water. I find so much joy in experiencing the diversity of food cultures when I visit different regions, each with their own special ingredients and flavours.

Among the numerous pickles made from leafy greens, three stand out as the most renowned: nozawana, takana and hiroshimana. The trio are collectively known as Japan's 'Three great leafy green pickles'. You may have heard of them.

These pickles can be enjoyed year-round. First, as asazuke – freshly pickled and vibrantly green. Later, as they undergo lactic acid fermentation, they develop a deeper flavour, or tang, and turn an amber hue; these pickles are known as furuzuke (aged pickles). Any green leafy vegetables work, even leaves you might usually put in the compost bin, such as radish, daikon and turnip leaves.

Traditionally, these greens are pickled only with salt, but adding seasoning liquid is a more modern interpretation that is also yummy.

1. Separate and thoroughly wash the green leafy vegetables, then drain. You'll need to sun-dry the leaves for 4–6 hours. I use clothes hangers and a clothesline for this, but you can also use a zaru (flat bamboo basket), colander or wire rack.
2. Remove the seeds from the chilli and finely slice it into rings. Finely slice the kombu.
3. When the vegetables have sun-dried, place them in a bowl and sprinkle over the salt, concentrating more on the stalks than the leafy tips. Massage the greens for 1–2 minutes.
4. Place the vegetables in a clean container, then add the kombu and chilli. Place an inner lid on top, followed by a weight at least twice as heavy as the vegetables. Pop a lid on top.
5. Within 1 day the vegetables will release enough liquid to submerge them. When this happens, lighten the weight just enough to keep them submerged, then cover them again. If the liquid hasn't risen by the next day, increase the weight slightly.

CONTINUED →

6. Allow the vegetables to rest in a cool, dark place for at least 3–4 days after the liquid has risen. You can eat the pickles now – in which case skip the rest of the steps. For a more modern approach, pickle the leaves in the pickling liquid.
7. Start by making the dashi. Soak the ingredients in the water and leave it overnight. The next day, pour the dashi into a bowl through a fine-mesh strainer and discard the umami elements (please use them for other purposes, such as making Kombu tsukudani – see page 244). You can skip this step and use store-bought dashi instead, if you like.
8. To make the pickling liquid, combine the ingredients in a saucepan and bring to the boil, then immediately remove from the heat and allow it to cool.
9. Remove the weight from the pickling container and squeeze the liquid from the leaves. Place the leaves in a clean container, then pour the cooled pickling liquid on top. Place an inner lid, then a weight just heavy enough to keep the vegetables submerged, then cover again. Allow the pickles to rest in a cool, dark place for at least 3–4 days before serving.
10. When serving, drain only the portion you plan to eat. Cut the pickles to your desired size and serve. Transfer any leftover pickles and liquid to a clean container and store in the refrigerator.

— *NOTES*: Vegetables from the brassica family that have thick, wide leaves are ideal for this dish. The leafy parts can be used as a substitute for nori seaweed and wrapped around onigiri for a delicious twist. The stalks, which have a nice crunch, can be enjoyed as pickles with a bowl of rice or added to simmered dishes or stir-fries.

When using thinner vegetables such as mizuna, it's best to stick to the salting process only, as this preserves their crisp texture. Mizuna has a slight bitterness, so sprinkling katsuobushi (bonito flakes) as a garnish can make it more palatable.

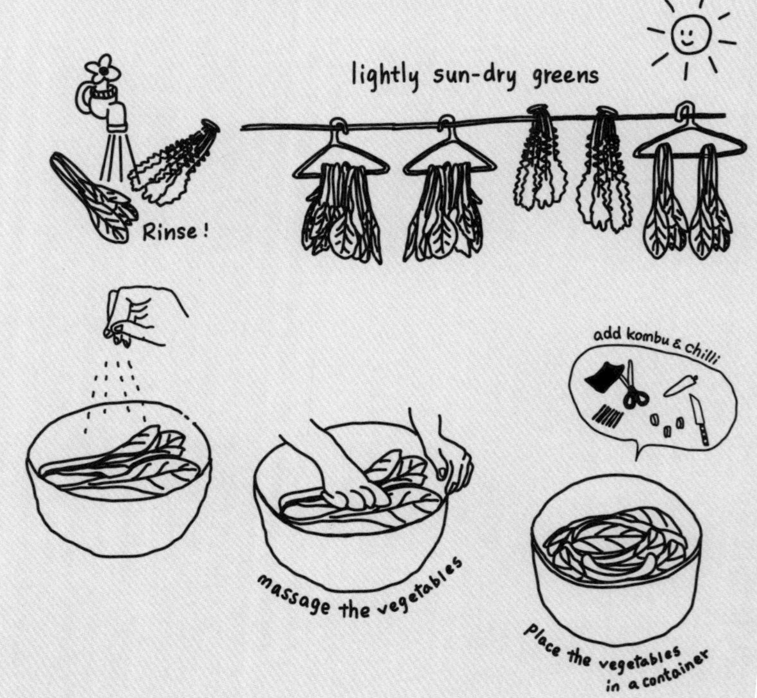

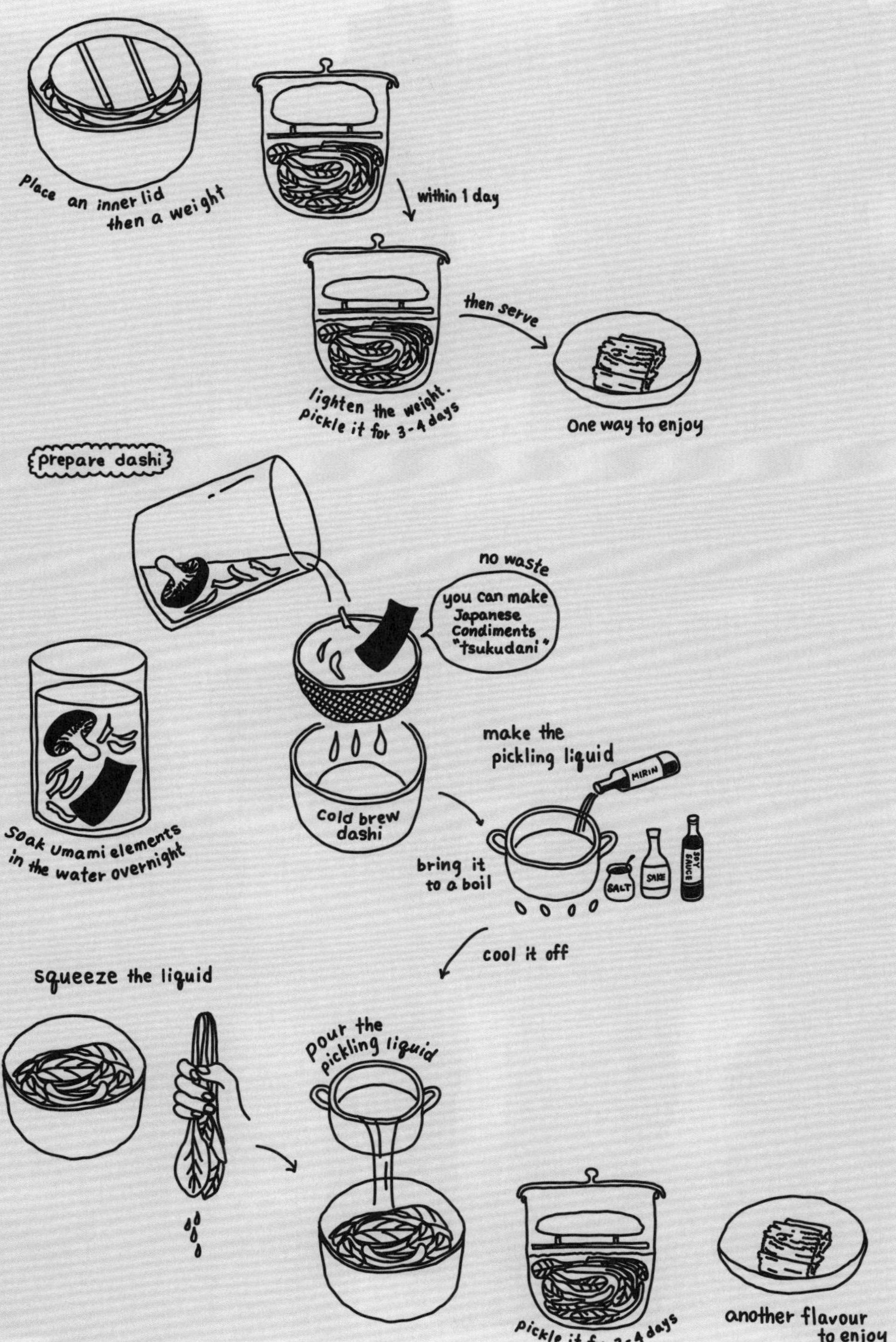
Place an inner lid then a weight
within 1 day
then serve
lighten the weight. pickle it for 3-4 days
One way to enjoy
prepare dashi
no waste
you can make Japanese Condiments "tsukudani"
Soak umami elements in the water overnight
Cold brew dashi
make the pickling liquid
MIRIN
bring it to a boil
SALT
SAKE
SOY SAUCE
cool it off
squeeze the liquid
pour the pickling liquid
pickle it for 3-4 days
another flavour to enjoy

HAKUSAI ZUKE

白菜漬け

FERMENTATION TIME:
4 days–1 month

Another traditional Japanese pickle that I absolutely adore is this hakusai zuke, or fermented wombok. I especially love the inner yellow parts of the vegetable. The flavour combination of lactic acid with the subtle sweetness and umami from the wombok, complemented by the elegant aroma of yuzu, is simply delightful. Yuzu brings such a beautiful fragrance and its vibrant colour brightens the stark, cold winter landscape when everything else seems to be in slumber. For me, yuzu is a happy tree and a celebration of winter.

In my family, our fermented wombok didn't include kombu. Our philosophy was to make use of what we had. All the pickling vegetables came from our garden, and we made pickles primarily for preservation. We never made a special trip to buy kombu just for pickling; it was always optional, and you can certainly make hakusai zuke without kombu or even without yuzu.

Hakusai zuke is so good with nabe (hotpot) – you almost don't need any other seasoning for the soup.

There are three steps in the traditional method: drying, pre-pickling and main fermentation.

CONTINUED →

1

SUN-DRYING THE WOMBOK

白菜の天日干し

Sun-drying is an essential step in the process of making hakusai zuke, as it enhances the flavour and preservation qualities of the wombok. By drying the wombok under the sun, excess moisture is removed and the leaves become softer. Sunlight activates the enzymes within the vegetable, bringing out its natural sweetness, which further enriches the flavour during fermentation. Additionally, sun-drying alters the cellular structure of the wombok, creating an environment where lactic acid bacteria can thrive. This ensures successful fermentation during pre-pickling and the main fermentation. Moreover, with reduced moisture, excessive liquid is less likely to seep out during the pickling process, preventing spoilage. It's a win–win in every way.

This recipe is for one wombok, but normally my family uses ten wombok to make hakusai zuke!

You will need
1 whole wombok (Chinese cabbage)
peel of 1 apple (optional)
peel of 1 persimmon (optional)

1. Remove two to three of the outer leaves from the wombok and put them aside.
2. Use a knife to score a cross in the bottom third of the base of the wombok, then tear it carefully into quarters by hand.
3. Make another score at the base of each quarter. This helps the pickling process and makes it easier to tear the wombok into halves when serving.
4. Place the wombok quarters and the outer leaves on a zaru (flat bamboo basket) or similar. Let the wombok dry for 4–5 hours in the sun or 1–2 days in the shade, until lightly wilted.
5. Dried apple or persimmon peels are often used to add aroma. If you'd like to add them to your hakusai zuke, peel the fruit and place the peels on the zaru. Leave them to dry outside in a sheltered place until they are either half-dried or fully dried. It's up to you.

CONTINUED →

2 PRE-PICKLING

下漬け

Pre-pickling is a short-term process that serves as a preparatory step for fermenting the wombok. By sprinkling salt over the wombok and lightly curing it, excess moisture is drawn out. Reducing the moisture allows the cabbage to be packed more compactly and efficiently into the pickling container. This step also helps to eliminate the raw, grassy odour (we call it 'green smell' in Japanese for some reason) and slight bitterness of the wombok before fermentation begins. Additionally, it suppresses the growth of harmful bacteria, creating a stable foundation for the overall quality of the pickles.

You will need
1 sun-dried wombok
salt (2.5% of dried wombok weight)

1. Weigh the dried wombok to determine the salt required.
2. Sprinkle some of the salt in the base of a large container.
3. Peel back the wombok quarters and sprinkle salt between each leaf, concentrating more salt at the base than the leafy tips.
4. Tightly pack a layer of wombok into the bottom of the container, alternating the tips and bases in opposite directions. Make sure not to leave any gaps. Sprinkle more salt on top.
5. Make another layer of wombok and sprinkle more salt on top. (If you have more wombok, repeat the process again.)
6. Use the outer leaves of the wombok to cover the top and sprinkle with the remaining salt.
7. Add an inner lid, followed by a weight at least twice as heavy as the dried wombok. Cover with a lid. If the weight sticks out from the container and the lid doesn't sit properly, cover the container with a plastic bag and newspaper, securing it tightly to keep out dust and debris.
8. Allow the wombok to rest in a cool place for 1 day. The wombok will release enough liquid to just submerge it. If liquid hasn't risen above the wombok, increase the weight slightly and wait another day.

3 MAIN FERMENTATION

本漬け

The main fermentation for hakusai zuke focuses on developing flavour and enhancing preservation. By pickling the wombok with ingredients, such as kombu, chillies and fruit peels, the wombok absorbs rich and complex flavours. Over time, lactic acid bacteria become active, creating the characteristic tanginess and deep umami flavour unique to fermented pickles.

You will need

salt (0.5% of pre-pickled wombok weight)
1 pre-pickled wombok
2 dried chillies
5 cm (2 in) square of dried kombu, finely sliced (optional)
peel of 1 apple, sun-dried (optional)
peel of 1 persimmon, sun-dried (optional)
peel of 1 yuzu (optional)

1. Sprinkle some salt in the base of a large clean container.
2. Lightly squeeze the liquid from each piece of pre-pickled wombok. Weigh the wombok, then measure the salt based on the weight.
3. Tightly pack a layer of wombok in the new container. Sprinkle some salt, a chilli and some of your chosen flavouring ingredients on top, then repeat. (You can add as many alternating layers as you need to use up all of your wombok.) Use the reserved outer leaves of the wombok to cover the top and sprinkle with the remaining salt.
4. Place an inner lid on top, followed by a weight equal to the weight of the sun-dried wombok (before pre-pickling). Cover with a lid. If the weight still sticks out from the container and the lid doesn't sit properly, cover the container with a plastic bag and newspaper, securing securing it tightly to keep out dust and debris.
5. Allow the wombok to rest in a cool place for at least 3 days – personally, I prefer it after a week of pickling. You'll notice the refreshing scent of yuzu (assuming you used one) when it's ready.
6. Take only the amount you want to eat from the container and lightly squeeze the wombok to remove the liquid. Tear the wombok in half using the score as guide, then cut it into 4 cm (1 ½ in) wide pieces and serve upright.

STORAGE: *Store in a cool, dark place for up to 1 month. The flavour will continue to develop – enjoy the changes!*

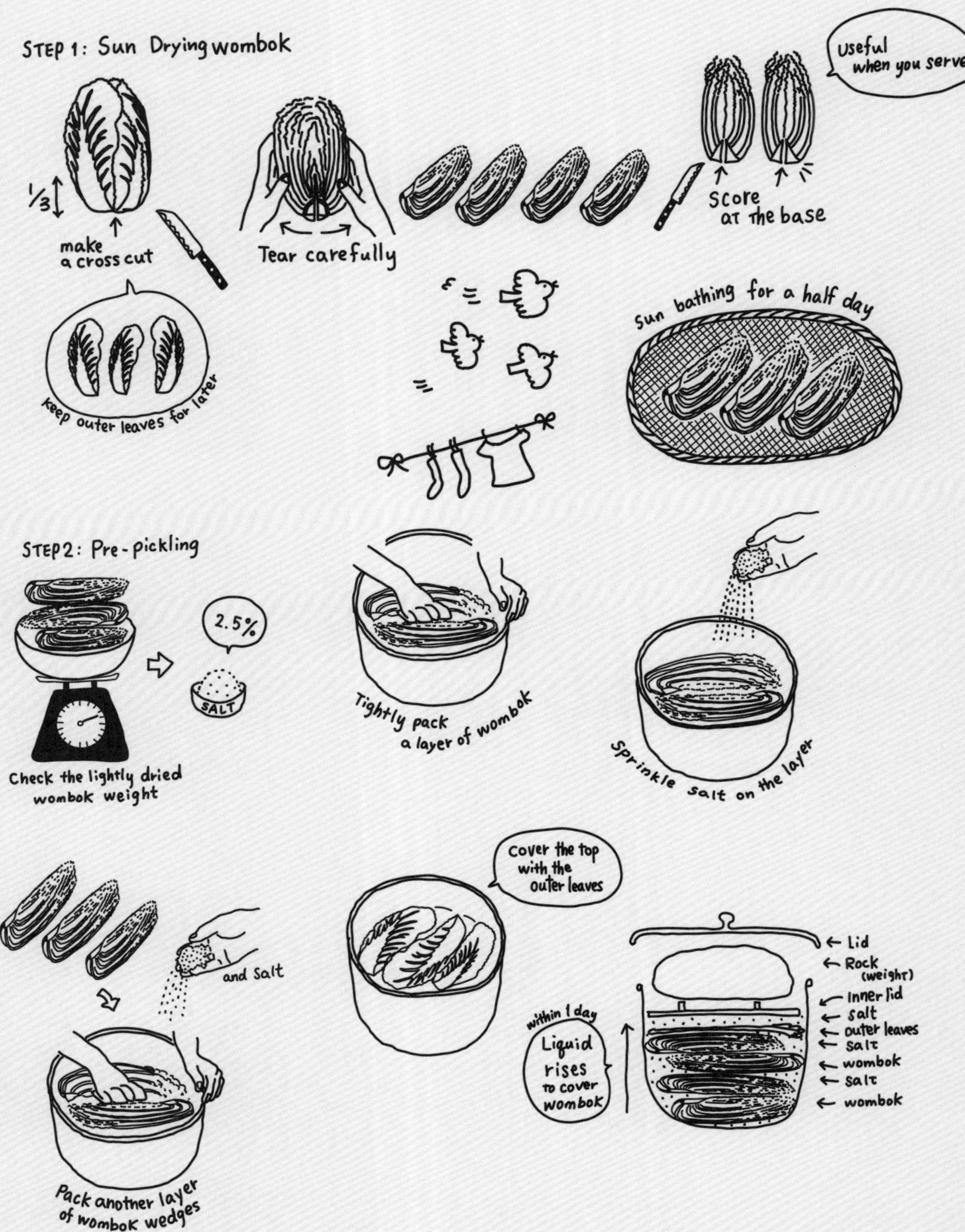
STEP 1: Sun Drying wombok
1/3
make a cross cut
Tear carefully
Score at the base
Useful when you serve
keep outer leaves for later
Sun bathing for a half day
STEP 2: Pre-pickling
2.5%
SALT
Check the lightly dried wombok weight
Tightly pack a layer of wombok
Sprinkle salt on the layer
and Salt
Pack another layer of wombok wedges
Cover the top with the outer leaves
within 1 day
Liquid rises to cover wombok
Lid
Rock (weight)
Inner lid
salt
outer leaves
salt
wombok
salt
wombok

STEP 3: Main pickling
Lightly squeeze
Check the wombok weight
0.5%
SALT
sprinkle salt at the bottom
Tightly pack a layer of wombok
Add some Aroma & umami element
apple peel
Yuzu skin
persimmon
Kombu
Chilli
Sprinkle some salt on top
Repeat the process if you have more wedges
Pack another layer of wombok wedges
Cover the top with outer leaves
Fermenting time
at least 3 days ~ 1 month
Half weight
make sure the rest of the wombok stays in the liquid
Take out only the amount you need
squeeze lightly
Carefully tear in half from the bottom part
serve it up right♡

AUNTY HARUKO'S HAKUSAI ZUKE

はるこおばちゃんの白菜漬け

FERMENTATION TIME:
4 days

You will need

1 pre-pickled wombok (Chinese cabbage; see pages 254–258)
salt (0.5% of pre-pickled wombok weight)

Filling

2 carrots
salt (2% of carrot weight)
3–4 Garlic tamarizuke (see page 216) or 1–2 garlic cloves
50 g (1¾ oz) shio (salted) kombu or regular dried kombu
70 g (2½ oz) tiny dried shrimp (sakura ebi)
90 g (3 oz) tiny dried sardines (jako)

STORAGE: *Store in a cool, dark place or in the refrigerator for up to 1 month. If you prefer furuzuke (aged pickles), store the hakusai zuke in the refrigerator for a further month.*

— *NOTE*: For a vegan version, replace the dried shrimp and sardines with dried mushrooms and colourful vegetables.

I got this recipe from my Aunty Haruko, who also taught me about miso pickling. She is my favourite! I always like to visit her or have her over to our house. I ask her all about the past – about the lifestyle, clothing, food, culture ... Aunty Haruko and I share similar tastes, and I have been fortunate enough to inherit all of her beautiful kimonos. We both like eating and she also shares her cooking knowledge and recipes, especially traditional flavours. This is her recommended hakusai zuke recipe, which includes various dried ingredients between the wombok layers. The umami from the dried ingredients combines with the lactic acid bacteria in the fermented wombok, resulting in a delicious dish. With all the dried ingredients added, it becomes quite a luxurious pickle.

1. Follow step 1 (sun-drying; page 257) and step 2 (pre-pickling; page 258) of the Hakusai zuke recipe to pre-pickle the wombok.
2. Remove the wombok from the container and lightly squeeze to remove the liquid. Weigh the wombok, then prepare the salt based on the weight. Set aside.
3. Julienne the carrots and place them in a bowl with the salt. Allow them to sit for 10 minutes, then use both hands to squeeze out the excess liquid. Julienne the garlic and finely slice the kombu.
4. Place the remaining filling ingredients in a bowl with the carrot garlic and kombu and combine well.
5. Peel back the wombok leaves and insert the filling between the leafy layers.
6. Tightly pack a layer of the filled wombok wedges into a clean container and sprinkle some of the salt on top. Tightly pack another layer and sprinkle with more salt, then finish with the outer wombok leaves.
7. Add an inner lid (or a plate) and a weight equal to the weight of the sun-dried wombok (before pre-pickling). Cover with a lid.
8. Allow the wombok to rest in a cool place for 3–4 days. Typically, it becomes even more delicious after about 1 week. Those living in warmer climates should let it ferment in the refrigerator.
9. To serve, take a wombok wedge and lightly squeeze to remove the liquid (be careful: you don't want to ruin all the beautiful mille-feuille layers). Cut the wedges into 4–5 cm (1½–2 in) thick slices, and arrange the layers upright on a plate.

Pre-pickled wombok
Keep the outer leaves
Lightly squeeze
Check the wombok weight
0.5%
SALT

Prepare fillings
carrot
Julienne
Salting
Squeeze
SHIO KOMBU
OR
Kombu
Dried prawn
JAKO
Dried tiny fish
Mix all filling ingredients
insert fillings in between layers

like a mille-feuille
sprinkle salt at the bottom
Tightly pack a layer of wombok
Sprinkle salt on the layer
Cover the top with outer leaves
Half weight
Take out only the amount you need
Leave the rest in the container
Don't drop any fillings
Gently squeeze lightly
make sure the rest of the wombok stays in the liquid
serve it upright

UME SHIGOTO

梅仕事

In Japan, the term *ume shigoto* translates to 'ume work'. It refers to the tasks performed when preserving ume during their harvest season (it's so busy!). Because ume cannot be eaten raw, they require processing. This involves various steps and activities to make the most of the ume, ensuring they can be enjoyed throughout the year.

The most famous way to preserve ume is to make umeboshi. It is the quintessential Japanese pickle. For most Japanese people, just thinking about umeboshi makes their mouth water – it's a reflex, likely because traditional umeboshi are quite sour and salty. Growing up, I was always told, 'Eat one umeboshi every day.' I used to finish my breakfast by popping half or a whole umeboshi into my mouth before leaving the table.

Umeboshi are often placed inside onigiri or added to the centre of a bento box packed with rice. The look of the rice with a single umeboshi in the centre is reminiscent of the Japanese flag (known as Hinomaru in Japanese), which is why these bento are called Hinomaru bento. Umeboshi have a preservative effect, helping prevent the rice in the bento from going bad. It makes them an essential component of bento and onigiri.

I personally see umeboshi as a kind of medicine. Whenever my stomach is upset, I eat one, and when I think I might get motion sickness, I tuck a few umeboshi into my bag. They are well known for their 'detoxifying' properties. In addition, umeboshi are often used to remove unpleasant smells from other ingredients and are frequently cooked with fish or meat. They also act as a flavour accent in many dishes. So, if you're interested in making Japanese food, making umeboshi yourself and keeping some on hand is a good idea.

The aroma of ume filling the room when they are ripening is utterly enchanting – such a delightful scent. The sight of salt sprinkled on the ume like falling snow is simply beautiful. When adding salted red shiso to the ume, the vibrant colour is breathtaking. Making umeboshi is an experience that stimulates all of my senses.

Other ume shigoto include ume jam, umeshu (plum wine), ume miso, ume shoyu, ume syrup, honey umeboshi ... There are so many ways we can preserve ume. It's a lot of work, but people know and appreciate all the effort that goes into creating the lovely ume produce that they enjoy for the rest of the year. That's probably why the term ume shigoto remains. Ume is the only fruit that has this specific term associated with it – it's testament to how special it is in Japanese culture.

Here I will introduce just a few of the many ume shigoto enjoyed throughout Japan.

MUM'S UMEBOSHI

母の梅干し

PICKLING TIME: *1 month*

You will need
as many ume (Japanese plums) as you can get!
salt (10% of ume weight)
red shiso leaves (20% of ume weight)

For sterilisation:
50–60 ml (1¾–2 fl oz) shochu (white liquor), brandy or vodka

STORAGE: *Store in a cool, dark place for up to 100 years or more!*

— *NOTES*: If you pickle the ume with 10% salt, mold should not form; however, shake the container daily at steps 5, 6 and 7 to move the liquid, which helps prevent mold developing. If you do observe any signs of mold, remove it and sprinkle the area with shochu.

If you want to avoid using shochu, use 15% salt instead.

I love sitting in the dining room with Mum and preparing ume for umeboshi together. The room is filled with an indescribably delightful aroma of ume, and it feels like every cell in my body is rejoicing – it's such a blissful moment, which ume brings once a year.

Freshly made umeboshi have a beautiful, vibrant red colour, but over the course of two or three years, their hue gradually changes and the saltiness mellows.

1. Go through all of the ume and remove any that are damaged as these can cause mold. Only use fully ripened, yellow ume. If any of the ume are green, leave them at room temperature for a few days to ripen. Use a toothpick to carefully remove the stalks from each ume. Soak the ume in a large container of water overnight. When ume are really ripe the soaking time can be only 1–2 hours.
2. The next day, drain the ume in a colander. Use a clean cloth or paper towel to carefully wipe the moisture off each one. Weigh the ume to calculate how much salt you will need.
3. Prepare the shochu by pouring it into a spray bottle. Spray the shochu inside a large clean container to sterilise it, then add a single layer of ume. Sprinkle a handful of salt over the ume, then lightly spray with the shochu.
4. Add another layer of ume, salt and shochu. Repeat this process, layer by layer, until all the ume have been used. Top with any remaining salt. Place an inner lid on top, followed by a weight equal to the weight of the ume. Add an outer lid and allow the ume to rest in a cool place.
5. Within about 2 days, the ume will release enough liquid to become submerged. When this happens, reduce the weight so it's just heavy enough to keep the ume fully submerged. (This is important. If you keep the heavy weight on, excess water will continue to be released from the ume, resulting in firm umeboshi, but if the ume don't remain fully submerged in the liquid, mold can develop easily, especially when pickling with this reduced amount of salt.)
6. The ume can now be stored in a cool place until the red shiso leaves are harvested (in summer) or become available at the market.
7. Once the red shiso becomes available, you can proceed to add it to the ume. First, pull the shiso leaves from the stems. Wash the leaves thoroughly and drain the excess water.

CONTINUED →

8. Take 100 ml (3½ fl oz) of the liquid, known as white umezu (shiro umezu), from the ume container and place it in a bowl. Use the liquid to gently massage the red shiso leaves until they soften and become floppy, and the liquid turns a dark reddish brown. Squeeze the leaves tightly to remove the liquid and discard the umezu.
9. Take 200 ml (7 fl oz) more white umezu from the ume container and place it in a bowl. Massage the red shiso leaves with the liquid again. This time, unlike the first, the white umezu should turn a beautiful red colour.
10. Transfer the massaged shiso leaves and the umezu to the ume container and gently mix to distribute the red liquid (it's fine to leave the red shiso leaves on top of the ume, too).
11. Place the inner lid back on with the weight to ensure all the ume are submerged in the umezu, then store in a cool place for 1–2 weeks, until the ume are red, inside and out.
12. Check the weather forecast to decide the best day for drying the ume. You must have three consecutive sunny days (no clouds – it can't be overcast) with no rain. This is important!
13. Gently remove the ume and red shiso leaves from the container and spread them on a zaru (flat bamboo basket) or a large, flat sieve. Leave the liquid, known as red umezu, in the container with the lid off to be sterilised by the sun, alongside the ume.
14. Leave the ume, shiso and pickling liquid to dry in the sun for 3 days and nights in a row. On the morning of the fourth day, at dawn when the umeboshi are still moist from the night dew, place all the ume and red shiso leaves into a clean container to store them. I use a ceramic pot with a lid for this. Transfer the liquid to a clean jar or bottle to use as red umezu for the rest of the year.
15. Sprinkle a little shochu on top of the umeboshi and red shiso as a final touch. Once you've done this, the umeboshi won't grow mold for many, many years.

Yoko's suggestion
仕込みの塩分濃度

Mum's recipe is made with 10 per cent salt. The umeboshi is made in the traditional way, but the amount of salt has been quite reduced compared to the amount traditionally used, which is more like 20 per cent. Twenty per cent is quite salty, but also quite safe – I mean, there's a lot less chance of it growing mold. So, if you are beginner, perhaps start with 18 per cent salt – a little bit salt-reduced, but enough to not have to worry about mold. Then, once you become comfortable making umeboshi, you can gradually reduce the amount of salt, if you want to.

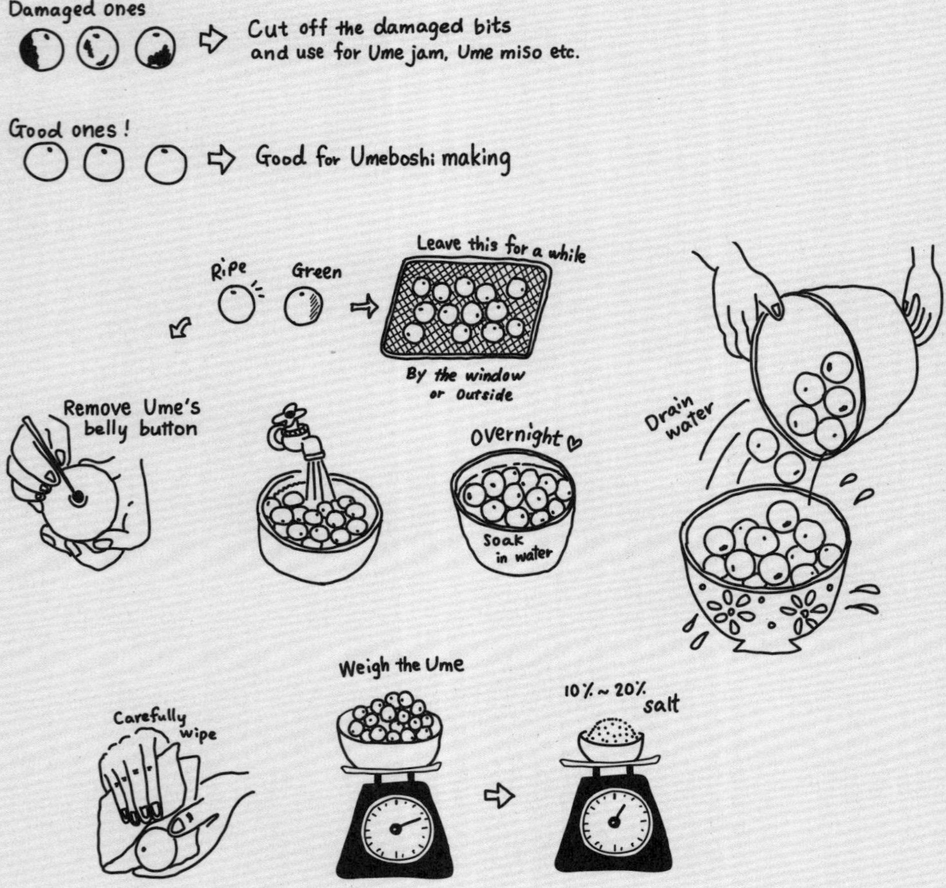

– *NOTES:* Ume are rich in citric acid, and when they're salted, osmosis draws out their moisture, creating a salty, tangy liquid known as ume vinegar. This vinegar is the essence of the citric acid and is considered a byproduct of the umeboshi-making process.

During umeboshi preparation, red shiso leaves may be added. The ume vinegar produced before adding the red shiso is called shiro umezu (white vinegar), while the vinegar after adding the red shiso is known as aka umezu (red vinegar). These two types of ume vinegar can be used according to preference and purpose.

The pickles made using ume vinegar are referred to as umezu zuke (pickled in ume vinegar). Red umezu is often used to give pickles a reddish hue (see pages 96–100), but it's important to note that it is considerably saltier than regular vinegar, so care should be taken with the amount used. It is also common to mix regular vinegar and ume vinegar in equal parts for a balanced flavour.

Pour Shochu into a spray bottle
SHO CHU
35%
Sterilise the Pickling Container
within 2 days!!
cover
weight
string
Inner Lid
salt
ume
salt
ume
salt
ume
salt
weight
Umezu
white ume vinegar
Red Shiso
Massage red shiso with Umezu
2 times
Add massged red shiso
Umezu
Now Red Ume Vinegar
Leave Ume & Umezu outside for 3 days & 3 nights
Red Umezu
Shiso as well
Transfer to storage container on the 4TH day's morning before sunrise!!
Final touch
spray Shochu
UMEZU

APRICOT UMEBOSHI

あんず干し

PICKLING TIME: *3 weeks*

You will need

apricots
salt (10% of apricot weight)
citric acid (1% of apricot weight; optional)
red shiso leaves (20% of apricot weight)

For sterilisation:
50–60 ml (1¾–2 fl oz) shochu (white liquor), brandy or vodka

STORAGE: *Store in the refrigerator for up to 1 year.*

While ume are readily available in Japan, there are many regions where they cannot be found. But don't worry, you can substitute them with apricots. I have two ume trees growing in my garden now, but before I acquired them I felt sad that I couldn't enjoy umeboshi. So, I decided to use the abundant apricots from my garden and, to my surprise, I ended up with a fruitier version of umeboshi. Of course, it's not exactly the same – especially in regards to its sourness and health benefits – but apricots can yield delicious results. You can also add citric acid to achieve the desired umeboshi sourness.

1. Simply substitute apricots for ume and follow the instructions for Mum's umeboshi on page 269.
2. If you would like to add extra sourness, weigh the apricots and add 1 per cent citric acid when you pickle them with the salt. That's all there is to it!

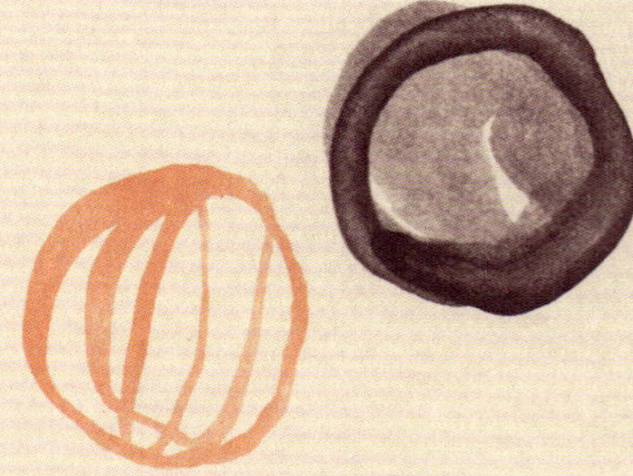

— *NOTE:* Apricots have softer flesh and contain more moisture than ume, which makes them slightly less stable in terms of preservation. The limit for storing apricot umeboshi at room temperature is around 1–2 months. For long-term storage, I recommend refrigerating them.

THE RISE OF THE NETWORK SOCIETY
EXPLODING THE PHONE

KARIKARI UMEZUKE

カリカリ梅

PICKLING TIME: *3 weeks*

You will need

green ume (Japanese plums)

salt (10% of ume weight)

red shiso leaves (20% of ume weight)

For sterilisation:

50–60 ml (1¾–2 fl oz) shochu (white liquor), brandy or vodka

STORAGE: *Store in the refrigerator for up to 3 months.*

'Karikari' is an onomatopoeia in Japanese that describes a crispy or crunchy texture. Umezuke is a version of umeboshi that isn't dried. By not drying the ume, you can preserve their crunchy texture. Unless you live in a cold area it's necessary to store the pickles in the refrigerator. Crunchy ume can be chopped with a knife for easier use.

1. To make karikari ume, follow the instructions for Mum's umeboshi on page 269, but use green, unripe ume.
2. Make a few cuts in each ume before salting them to ensure they turn a beautiful red all the way through to the core.
3. After adding the red shiso, the process is complete. (There's no drying.)
4. Store them in the refrigerator submerged in red umezu.
5. To serve, add them to onigiri or bento or enjoy as tapas.

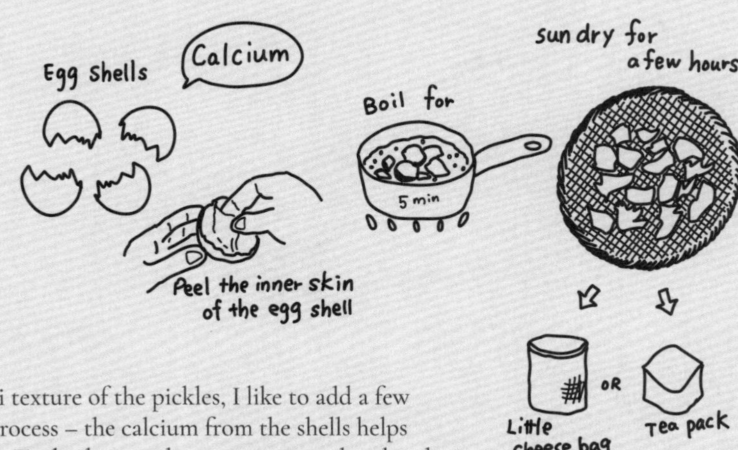

Yoko's suggestion

カリカリを長持ちさせるために

To help maintain the karikari texture of the pickles, I like to add a few eggshells during the salting process – the calcium from the shells helps maintain the crunchy texture. To do this, crack two eggs into a bowl and use the eggs in another dish. Peel the inner skin from the shells, then boil the eggshells for 5 minutes, drain and allow to dry in the sun for 2 hours. Transfer the eggshells to a small cotton bag or empty tea pouch and add to the ume jar when you add the salt.

Storing karikari ume in the freezer will also help maintain their crunchy texture for longer.

UMESHU PLUM WINE

梅酒

PICKLING TIME:
2–3 months

You will need
1kg (2 lb 3 oz) green ume
500 g–1 kg (1 lb 2 oz–2 lb 3 oz) rock sugar (candy sugar)
1.8 litres (61 fl oz) shochu (white liquor) or sake

STORAGE: *Store the umeshu in a cool, dark place for many years.*

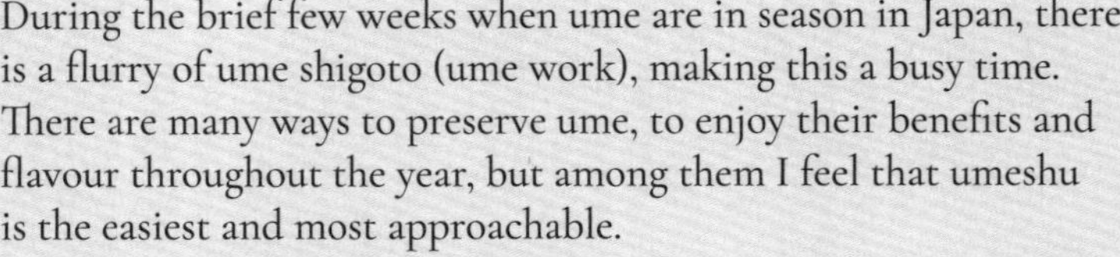

During the brief few weeks when ume are in season in Japan, there is a flurry of ume shigoto (ume work), making this a busy time. There are many ways to preserve ume, to enjoy their benefits and flavour throughout the year, but among them I feel that umeshu is the easiest and most approachable.

Umeshu is typically made with unripe green ume, resulting in a clear and crisp finish. However, fully ripened ume can also be used. When made with ripe ume, the liquid becomes cloudy and develops a slightly thicker, more velvety texture. In both cases, enjoying a soaked ume with the infused alcohol is one of the delights of umeshu.

After about a year, remove the ume from the jar – the umeshu will continue to mature over time, developing an even smoother and more refined flavour.

1. Discard any damaged ume. Rinse the ume under running water, gently rubbing them with your palms to avoid damaging the fruit. Drain in a colander.
2. Use a clean cloth or paper towel to wipe each ume dry, then use a toothpick to remove the stalks. Wipe away any remaining moisture from the area.
3. Place a layer of ume in a large sterilised jar and scatter over a layer of rock sugar. Repeat to create 3–4 layers. Gently pour in the shochu or sake, then cover with a lid.
4. Store the jar in a cool, dark place for 2–3 months, gently shaking the jar once a week to help the ingredients blend and the sugar dissolve.
5. To serve, pour some umeshu over ice, add a soaked ume and enjoy. The umeshu will keep for many years.

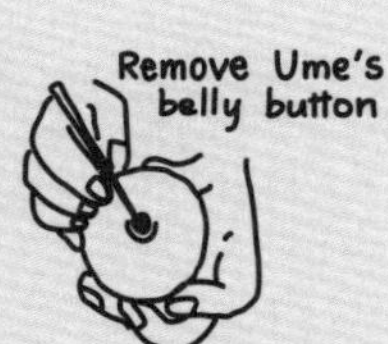

THANK YOU

あとがき

Thank you for picking up *The Japanese Art of Pickling & Fermenting.* I hope you find even just one tip, insight or favourite recipe in this book that enriches your heart and daily life. The pickles featured here have been lovingly made and passed down through generations in Japanese homes and communities.

I am grateful to the ancestors who have honoured nature and continued the tradition of pickling through the seasons.

I wish that your pickling journey is both delicious and enjoyable. I also hope this book will be cherished for many years to come.

Autumn 2025
Yoko Nakazawa なかざわ ようこ

To my parents in Japan: thank you for always supporting me with warmth and care. When I was young, I played around the garden, and the vegetables harvested from that garden would be turned into delicious meals on our table ... Those everyday experiences and the way of life that cherishes old traditions have formed the foundation of this book. I am truly grateful. There is still so much I want to learn from both of you. Please continue to stay healthy and happy. And to Kesako-san, thank you for continually helping me, no matter how many times I asked about recipes. Your contribution was huge.

To Aunty Haruko: thank you for always sharing such fascinating stories with me. I'm so grateful that I was able to include the miso pickles you always said were delicious – the ones sent from the countryside – in this book. Your detailed guidance meant so much to me. Also, the kimono you passed down to me looked so happy during the photoshoot!

Once you're feeling better, let's go to that sushi bar again.

To the incredible team behind this book: first and foremost, I would like to express my heartfelt gratitude to Paul McNally at Smith Street Books for giving me this incredible opportunity. I am also deeply thankful to Brendan Liew for recommending me. As someone devoted to food, publishing a cookbook has been a long-cherished dream. Now that this dream has become a reality, looking back on the journey, I realise how every step of the process has been an invaluable experience. It has also reaffirmed to me that creating a book is truly a labour of love, made possible by the dedication and effort of so many people. One of the most memorable moments for me was after the photoshoot, when the team picked up the pickles and tasted them. It was both nerve-wracking and deeply rewarding to see those reactions. As a fellow book lover, I sincerely hope that you will continue to bring many more wonderful books into the world.

To editor, Martine Lleonart: I can only imagine how challenging it must have been to grasp the meaning I wanted to convey, envision it, and then shape it into a cohesive piece of writing. For me, our exchanges felt like corresponding with a pen pal in the past – an experience that was both enjoyable and heart-warming. Thank you.

To photographer Rochell Eagle and food stylist Meryl Batlle: I was constantly in awe of your incredible teamwork, dedication and the outstanding quality of your work. Having the opportunity to collaborate with you both was truly a valuable experience for me. Thank you for never saying no and for being willing to try different approaches. The stunning photographs you created are a joy to look at time and time again. I am truly grateful.

To designer Michelle Mackintosh: thank you so much for creating such a beautiful design, from the cover to every detail inside! Everyone on the team was absolutely in love with your talent. I'm truly delighted for how your exceptional design has made this book truly shine.

To Managing Editor Lucy Heaver: your presence, always bringing positive energy to the team, was truly reassuring. Thank you for handling this non-regular style with great patience and persistence. I'm deeply grateful for your dedication in helping to bring this beautiful book to life.

Dear lovely friends, thank you all so much for your constant support and love. Anna and Symon, for giving such strong support and cheering me on with the book; Emma, for providing beautiful tableware, but also for being a wonderful mentor and friendly neighbour; Patrick and Rachel, for offering help during the writing process and for sharing your honest thoughts; Chris and Sam, for always checking in on the progress; Rachel, for being the best neighbour to talk to about the book; Andrew, for being my Japanese food and sake friend, also for sharing your perspective on books; Chinatsu, for being such a strong support and helping me with Japanese language queries as an experienced translator.

Billy, thank you for teaching me about this industry and what it means to publish a book, to an absolute beginner. Your guidance was incredibly reassuring. I also respect you as a firefighter.

Mandy, founder of Global Sisters (https://globalsisters.org/), thank you for always checking in on the progress of the book. As a migrant woman, the fact that I was able to start my miso business and continue it to this day is undoubtedly thanks to the guidance and encouragement of Global Sisters. It is through you and your team's continuous support that I was given the opportunity to publish this book. I am deeply grateful for your unwavering commitment.

Last but not least, my dear husband, Hugh Davies: for over 10 years, you have continually encouraged me to write a book. You've always been my greatest partner, and during the hectic times of writing and preparing all the pickles, you patiently supported me with warmth and love. I am truly grateful from the bottom of my heart.

Contributions of Ceramics

Emma Jimson (Pom-me-granite studio) https://www.pommegranite.com.au/: Cabbage bowl (P91), Cat chopsticks rest (P255), Origami series bowl (P278); Anna Forsyth: Little Umeboshi pot (P270); Ginza Takumi http://www.ginza-takumi.co.jp/: (P92, P255). Thank you for your kind advice about ceramics.

『The Japanese Art of PICKLING & FERMENTING』
を手にとってくださり、ありがとうございます。

この本の中に、一つでも皆様の心や暮らしを豊かにするヒントやひらめき、そしてお気に入りのレシピが見つかれば嬉しいです。ここで紹介するお漬物は、日本の家庭や地域で長く作り継がれ、愛されてきたものです。自然を敬い、季節とともにお漬物を受け継いできた先人たちに感謝を込めて。また、皆様のお漬物作りが、美味しく楽しいものになりますように。この本が長く愛されることを願って。

2025 秋　　なかざわ　ようこ

日本で暮らす両親へ　いつも温かく見守っていてくれて、ありがとう。小さい頃、畑のまわりで遊び、その畑で採れた野菜が美味しい料理となって食卓に並ぶ…そんな日々の積み重ねや、昔ながらのしきたりを大切にする暮らしが、この本の原点になりました。心から感謝しています。そして、けさこさん。何度もレシピを聞く私に、懲りることなく協力してくれて、本当にありがとう。まだまだ二人から教えてもらいたいことがたくさんあります。どうか、これからも元気でいてください。

はるこおばちゃん

いつも興味深いお話を聞かせてくれて、ありがとう。おばちゃんが「美味しい」と言っていた、田舎から送られてくる味噌漬けを、この本に掲載することができました。細かく教えてくれて、本当に感謝しています。それから、おばちゃんから譲り受けた着物たちも、写真撮影の時、とても嬉しそうでした！

Smith Street Booksをはじめ、この出版に関わってくださったプロフェッショナルチームの皆さん、素敵な本にしてくださり本当にありがとうございました。また、家族、友人、多くの人のサポート・協力がございまして、ここまで辿り着くことができました。この場を借りて心より御礼申し上げます。

INDEX

Smith Street Books

Published in 2025 by
Smith Street Books
Naarm (Melbourne) | Australia
smithstreetbooks.com

Distributed outside of ANZ,
North & Latin America by
Thames & Hudson Ltd.,
6–24 Britannia Street,
London, WC1X 9JD
thamesandhudson.com

EU Authorised Representative:
Interart S.A.R.L.
19 rue Charles Auray, 93500
Pantin, Paris, France
productsafety@thameshudson.co.uk; www.interart.fr

ISBN: 978-1-9232-3913-5

Smith Street Books respectfully acknowledges the Wurundjeri People of the Kulin Nation, who are the Traditional Owners of the land on which we work, and we pay our respects to their Elders past and present.

Publisher: Lucy Heaver
Editor: Martine Lleonart
Design, layout and watercolours: Michelle Mackintosh
Photographer: Rochelle Eagle
Food stylist: Meryl Batlle
Proofreader: Pamela Dunne
Indexer: Max McMaster
Prepress: Megan Ellis
Production manager: Aisling Coughlan

Printed & bound in China by C&C Offset Printing Co., Ltd.

Book 403
10 9 8 7 6 5 4 3 2